DISCOVER
CENTRAL AND WEST AFRICA

Reader's
Digest

PUBLISHED BY THE READER'S DIGEST ASSOCIATION LIMITED

LONDON   NEW YORK   MONTREAL   SYDNEY

DISCOVER CENTRAL AND WEST AFRICA

Translated and edited by Toucan Books Limited, London
for Reader's Digest, London
Translated and adapted from the French
by Andrew Kerr-Jarrett

For Reader's Digest
Series Editor: Christine Noble
Editorial Assistant: Lucy Murray
Prepress Accounts Manager: Penny Grose

Reader's Digest General Books
Editorial Director: Cortina Butler
Art Director: Nick Clark

First English language edition Copyright © 2002
The Reader's Digest Association Limited
11 Westferry Circus, Canary Wharf, London E14 4HE
www.readersdigest.co.uk

Reprinted with amendments 2004

We are committed to both the quality of our products and
the service we provide to our customers. We value your
comments, so please feel free to contact us on 08705 113366,
or by email at cust_service@readersdigest.co.uk
If you have any comments about the content of our books,
you can contact us at gbeditorial@readersdigest.co.uk

ISBN 0 276 42520 0

Discover the World: CENTRAL AND WEST AFRICA
was created and produced by
Hubert Deveaux & Co, Paris for
Selection Reader's Digest S.A., Paris, and first published in
2001 as *Regards sur le Monde: L'AFRIQUE DES SABLES ET DES FORÊTS*

©2001 Selection Reader's Digest, S.A.
212 boulevard Saint-Germain, 75007, Paris

CONTENTS

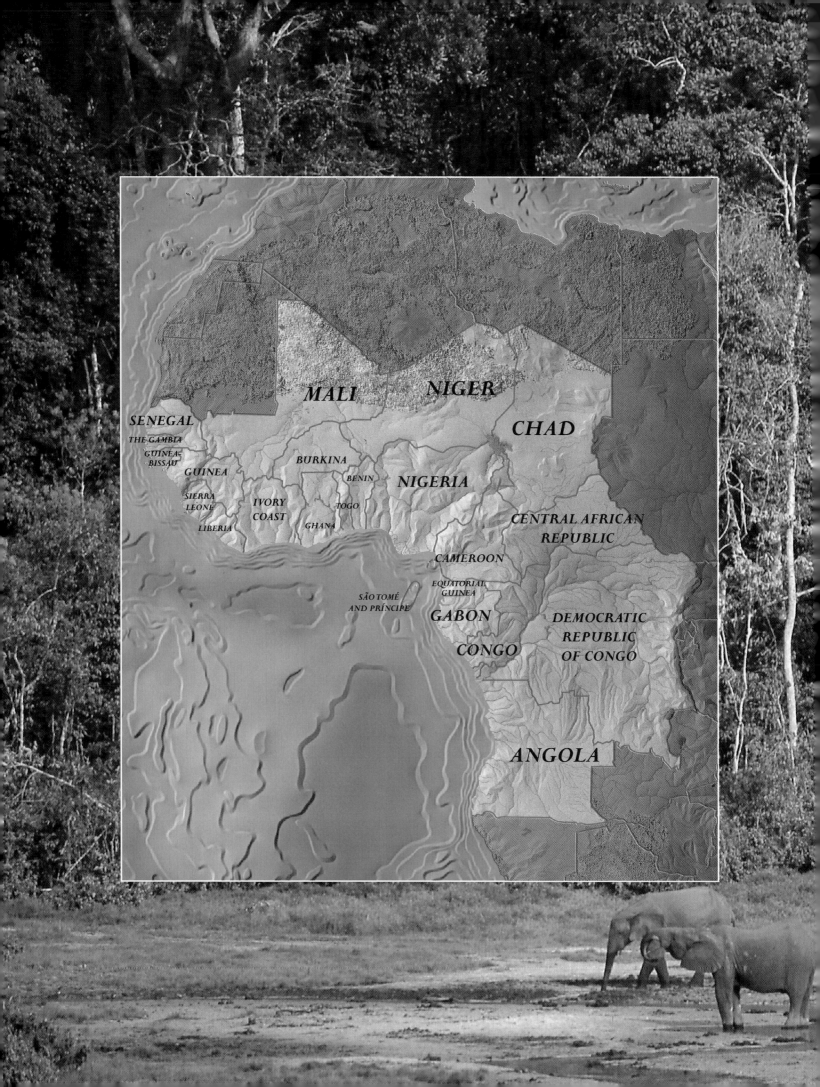

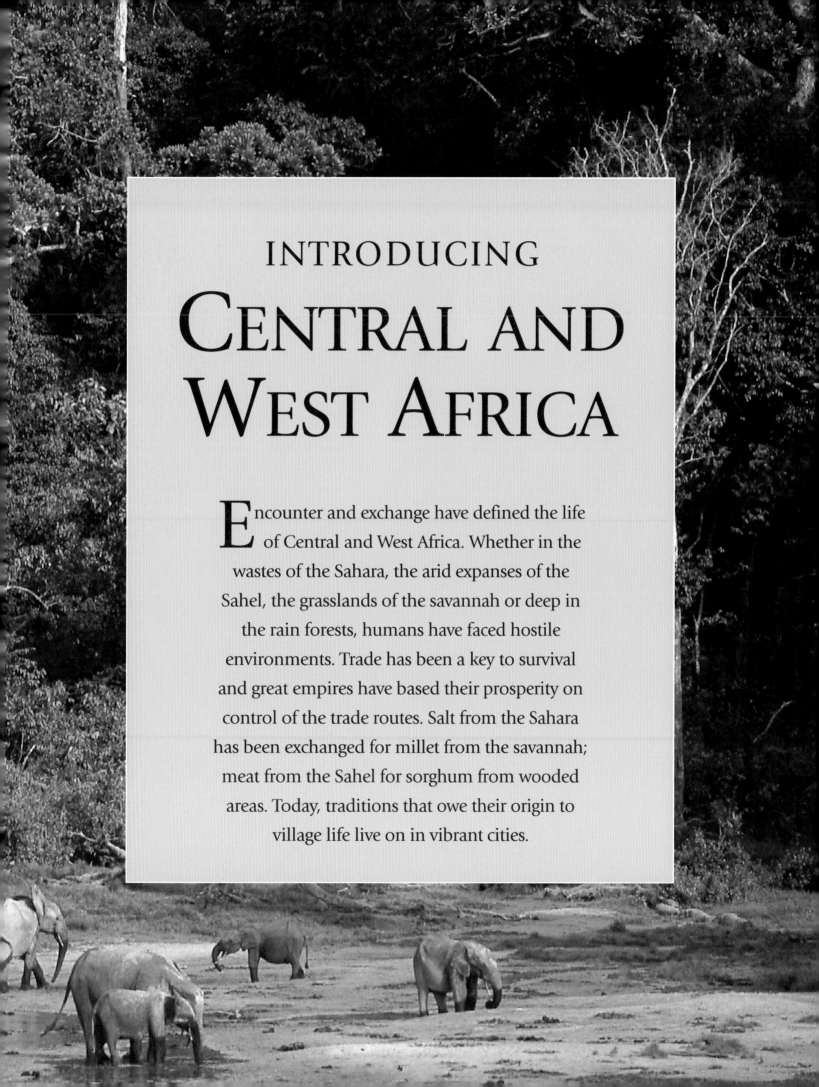

INTRODUCING
CENTRAL AND WEST AFRICA

Encounter and exchange have defined the life of Central and West Africa. Whether in the wastes of the Sahara, the arid expanses of the Sahel, the grasslands of the savannah or deep in the rain forests, humans have faced hostile environments. Trade has been a key to survival and great empires have based their prosperity on control of the trade routes. Salt from the Sahara has been exchanged for millet from the savannah; meat from the Sahel for sorghum from wooded areas. Today, traditions that owe their origin to village life live on in vibrant cities.

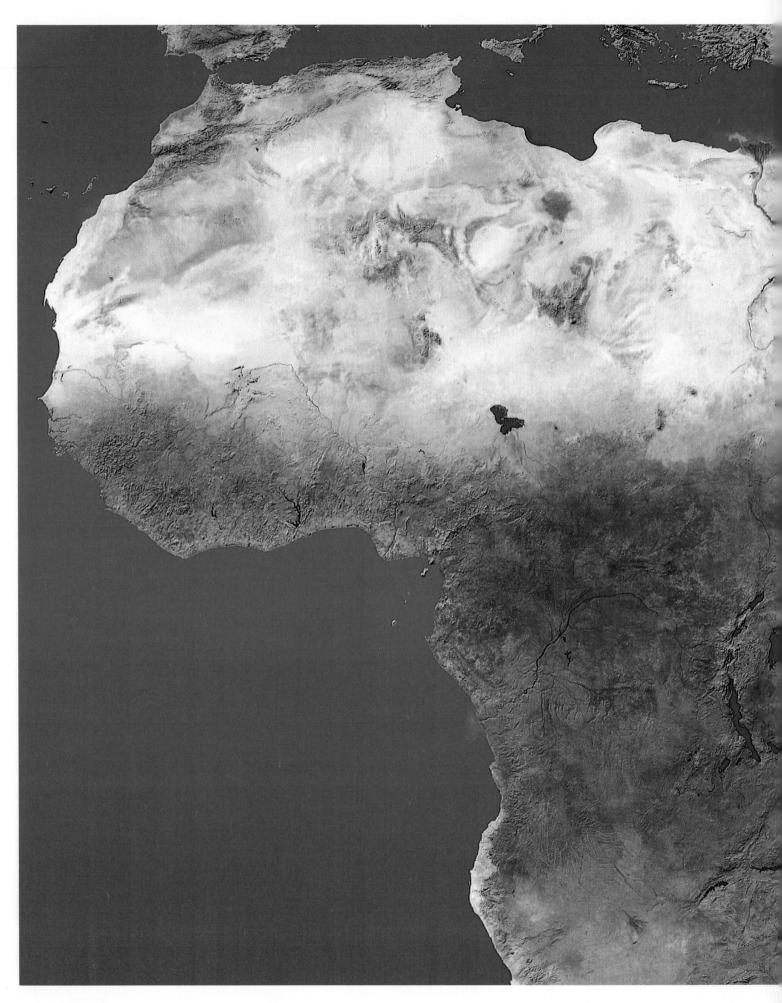

In desert and rain forest

West Africa stretches from parched desolation in the world's greatest desert, the Sahara, to dripping humidity in equatorial rain forests. The arid landscapes of its northern zone gradually give way to open savannah grasslands. Towards the Guinea coast, where moist air blows in from the Atlantic, rainfall levels increase. They rise, too, towards the interior of the continent. The savannah becomes dotted with bushes and trees, and eventually is replaced by rain forest.

Central Africa, straddling the Equator, is contained within the Congo basin, draining the waters of the entire vast rain-forest region. The zone has a humid climate with relentlessly high temperatures. To the east, the Congo basin rises to the ridge of high plateaus that separate it from the Nile basin and Great Rift Valley of East Africa. Dominating these tablelands is a series of volcanic peaks, born of the tectonic collision that created the Great Rift Valley. The largest active volcano is Nyiragongo, with impressive cable-like twists of lava emerging from its crater.

The Congo's main tributaries, mighty waterways in their own right, include the Sangha and Ubangi, which flow into it from the northern edges of the basin, and the Lomami, joining it from the south. In the west, the Congo tumbles over the rim of its basin in a succession of rapids and cataracts before reaching the Atlantic.

Most of the region's more northerly rivers, including the Sénégal, the Niger and the various rivers that flow into Lake Chad, have been affected by the creeping southward expansion of the Sahara, which began nearly 6000 years ago. Peoples, too, were forced to adapt. Driven from their Saharan homelands by drought, herders and farmers settled in the regions to the

Seen from above The transition from desert to greener regions to the south stands out clearly in a satellite photograph. Slicing through the zone of intersection is the arc of the River Niger and to the east lies Lake Chad. The Congo forms its own huge arc through the heart of the continent.

south, where around 2500 years ago they established early civilisations, such as the Djenné-Jeno culture in Mali and the Sao culture in Chad. These foreshadowed the splendour of the great empires of the savannah, including those of Ghana and Kanem.

While some of the migrating peoples settled in the savannahs, others took refuge in mountain regions. Communities grew up around the sheltered waters of coastal lagoons, protected from the ocean by sandbars. In the rain forests, other groups made clearings where they built their homes and grew their crops. Cultural and trade links grew up among these different peoples of the desert, savannah, forest and river valley. Then, around 2000 years ago, a new culture emerged in the region around Mont Cameroun, between West and Central Africa. Led by blacksmith kings, the Bantu peoples spread south, establishing new kingdoms in the forests, savannahs and deserts of southern Africa.

Despite the growth of the Sahara, which has reduced large parts of West Africa to desert or semidesert, huge grassland plains survive. They provide grazing for livestock – and their peoples increasingly provide labour for the cities, for the timber industry and for the plantations growing cocoa, cotton, bananas and other crops of the forest zones. Conflicts often arise between the savannah and forest peoples, usually as a result of clashing political and economic interests. Yet the fact remains that the two are interdependent. The forests have rich agricultural potential as well as diamonds, oil and other mineral resources, but these cannot be exploited without the workers from the poorer savannah regions.

More than ever, the key to survival lies in the ability of the people from different zones to work together. When faced with climatic or other kinds of pressure, communities in this part of Africa have learned to respond by changing their way of life. Nowadays, the pressure is at least as much social as climatic: the pressure on societies that were once predominantly rural to come to terms with urban life.

Rock and sand The sands of the Ténéré desert flow like melted milk chocolate over the edges of the Aïr massif, north-east of Agadez in the republic of Niger. The massif's highest points, the twin peaks of Bagzane (6634 ft/2022 m), command majestic views over granite summits and deep, steep-sided valleys, where some scrubby vegetation survives, including a few ancient olive trees.

Tree of many bounties The usefulness of the baobab tree is legendary. Its fruit, known as monkey bread, can be eaten as it is or made into a mildly acidic, refreshing drink. The leaves are dried, crushed and added as flavouring to the otherwise tasteless millet porridge, the staple of most savannah communities. And the hollow trunks of old trees are the traditional burial place of village bards, or griots.

The winding river Between Mopti and Timbuktu (Tombouctou) in Mali, the River Niger loses itself in a labyrinth of meanders. Only the Sorko people, traditional fishers and goods carriers, know how to find their way through this watery maze. When the river level is high, great masses of sedges and reeds clog the banks of the watercourses, impeding access to villages that have become islands.

9

The hunted hunters Hunting has reduced the numbers of leopards – known locally as panthers. Like lions, they are most likely to be seen in parks and reserves in areas of open savannah woodland. Local herders fear them because they prey on stray or injured animals from their flocks and herds.

Getting goodness from the ground A giraffe and some Derby eland lick the ground for essential mineral salts. Derby eland are the largest of the antelopes, the males weighing over 1300 lb (600 kg). They were a popular prey for game hunters and are now rare in West Africa, where they are mostly confined to national parks and game reserves, such as Senegal's Niokolo Koba park and Mali's Fine reserve. In Central Africa, they still roam parts of Chad, the Central African Republic and Cameroon.

Feeding and resting White pelicans enjoy the wetland riches of Djoudj National Bird Sanctuary in northern Senegal. About 60 miles (100 km) upstream from the mouth of the Sénégal river, on its southern bank, the sanctuary is home to around 150 bird species, including marabou storks, crowned cranes, African spoonbills, pink flamingos, herons, garganey ducks, northern pintail ducks – and countless seagulls wheeling overhead. Terns are elegant winter visitors.

10

A grove of giants Baobab trees are common in Senegal and across large parts of the western end of West Africa. Their seeds have a hard, thick outer layer, the 'coat', which needs to be broken open before they are able to germinate. This can happen inside the stomachs of the animals that feed on them. In this way, the livestock of Fulani herders carried the baobab eastwards across the region as, over the centuries, the Fulani themselves spread east.

Green haven in a parched land In the Dogon plateau of central Mali, most of the little rain that falls seeps away through the dry earth. In some places, however, farmers have built dams or ponds to catch the water; in others, natural depressions in the ground trap it and keep it. Where this happens, bands of vegetation, known as gallery forest, grow up on either side of the watercourse, attracting birds and small game.

Back to nature In the highlands of Ghana, the low shrubs of bush savannah give way to the denser growth of wooded savannah. Here, itinerant farmers clear vegetation to grow their crops. The topsoil is too poor, however, to sustain agriculture for any length of time. The farmers move on, and the clearing reverts to forest or grass. Grazing livestock disturb the shallow root systems of much of the vegetation.

The green and the brown *A wisp of cloud hangs over a river valley in the mountains of northern Cameroon. It is the rainy season and the river is flowing in full, muddy brown spate, crashing over a cliff edge in spectacular waterfalls.*

The saddle of Africa *The Ruwenzori range is the highest point in the ridge of mountains that form the watershed between the Nile and Congo basins. Although close to the Equator, its loftiest peaks – more than 16 400 ft (5000 m) above sea level – are permanently snow-covered. Below the snow line comes a zone of open tussocky meadows, which gives way lower down to the strange world of montane forest (right), where giant groundsels grow to be 40 ft (12 m) tall, ferns are trees and moss clings to everything. Lower again are cultivated areas, chiefly tea and coffee plantations, benefiting from a high annual rainfall of 157-236 in (4-6 m).*

Forest canopy *Tropical rain forest, its upper branches intertwining into a canopy, still covers huge swathes of the north-eastern part of the Democratic Republic of Congo and, farther west, much of Congo (Brazzaville) and Gabon.*

Cloud of spume *Atlantic waves crash onto the rocky shoreline of Boa Vista, the easternmost island of the Cape Verde archipelago. The islands are scattered like confetti, some 500 miles (800 km) off the coast of Senegal.*

The Guinea Coast *Long sandy beaches, interspersed with patches of mangrove, stretch for mile after mile along the West African shore – traditionally regarded as a dangerous coast for shipping. Behind the beaches is a band of dunes, and behind these stretch large lagoons, sheltered by the sandbar from the violence of the ocean waves. It is around these more tranquil waters that local people build their villages, making a living as fishers and farmers of the fertile* barre *soil (from the Portuguese* barro, *meaning 'clay') of the coastal plain.*

In full spate *Several rivers flow into the Saloum delta on the Senegalese coast between Dakar and the mouth of the Gambia river. They create a spectacular maze of waterways and rapids, bordered by forests and mangrove swamps, and are rich in fish, shellfish and birdlife.*

17

A brief history

Most researchers agree that Africa was the cradle of the human race. Remains of the toolmaker *Homo habilis*, a direct ancestor of humankind, were found in East Africa in the 1960s and the 3 million-year-old bones of an even earlier ancestor, the man-like ape 'Lucy' were discovered in Ethiopia in 1974. Modern man, *Homo sapiens sapiens*, evolved some 300 000 years ago and, driven by a constant need to find new sources of food, began the slow but relentless process of spreading across the face of the Earth.

About 12 000 years ago, for reasons not yet fully understood, the last Ice Age began to end. With glaciers and ice sheets melting and sea levels rising, rainfall became both more abundant and more widespread. Rivers began to flow in the vastness of the Sahara, lakes started to form, and grass and other plants began to flourish. Herds of large mammals, including elephants, giraffes, rhinoceroses and hippopotamuses, moved in from the south to take advantage, followed by the most opportunistic mammals of all – human beings. Evidence for the existence of the wild animals comes from fossilised bones and from rock paintings and engravings found in most of the mountain ranges of the Sahara. Of the people who made these prehistoric works of art we know little – except that they lived by hunting, fishing and gathering.

Between 7000 and 6000 BC, the Saharan climate changed yet again. Lakes and rivers in the northern part of the region dwindled or dried up altogether and the herds of game began to return south. Even so, the zone that includes northern Mauritania, Mali, Niger and Chad was still savannah, rather than the desert it is today. Rock paintings from this period, preserved for centuries in the dry desert air, show people herding flocks, hunting with bow and arrows and performing mysterious ceremonies. It is known as the Roundhead Period, after figures depicted wearing curious round bonnets.

When the grass grew green

Herdsmen and hunters, flocks and game, survived in the southern Sahara during the period 5500-4000 BC. Brilliantly coloured rock and cave paintings in the Ennedi massif of Chad show herders grazing long-horned cattle, probably originating from the Nile valley, on savannah grasslands. The paintings also depict archers. Together with finely crafted stone arrowheads, the

Fishing relic *This bone fish-hook was found in the delta of the Sénégal river, home to communities that lived by fishing and gathering shellfish.*

Rock memories *A giraffe engraved on rock in northern Chad bears witness to a time when big game were common in this part of the Sahara. Lake Chad was 20 to 30 times bigger than it is today, and mammals roamed its shores in large numbers.*

Earth mother *This small stone depiction of a mother-goddess was found on the peninsula of Cap Vert in Senegal. It is more than 2000 years old.*

Giraffe and hunter An archer carries his bow in a rock painting from the Aïr massif in Niger.
The bow would have been the principal weapon used by hunters living there more than 7000 years ago.

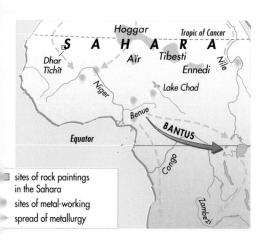

sites of rock paintings in the Sahara
sites of metal-working
spread of metallurgy

Large settlements grew up, some home to several thousand inhabitants, at places such as Dhar Tîchît in Mauritania. Sizable fishing communities established themselves on the banks of rivers and lakes and along the coast. By around 500 BC, however, the process of desertification had driven the last farmers out of the southern Sahara into the region known as the Sahel.

Arts of civilisation
The first civilisations of the savannahs arose among peoples who had mastered the skills of making pottery, working iron, raising livestock and cultivating crops. On the Benue plateau of Nigeria, a culture notable for its astonishingly lifelike terracotta figurines of animals and human heads flourished from around 500 BC. It is known as the Nok culture, after a tin-mining village where the first of these figurines were found in 1928. Djenné-Jeno, near modern Djenné in south-western Mali, emerged in the 3rd century BC as an important trading centre, thanks to its strategic position on an island in the River Bani at the southern end of the Niger's inland delta. Farther east, in the Lake Chad region, the Sao civilisation emerged in the 5th century AD.

In the Central African Republic to the south, farming communities as early as

paintings prove that hunting was an important activity for thousands of years.

By 4000 BC, the climate was becoming drier still, and whole regions of the central and southern Sahara became desert. Lakes evaporated, leaving expanses of briny water, where later generations would extract salt. The herders took refuge in the mountain ranges of the Sahara, where rainfall was higher, or headed south.

The scarcity of water meant that people who stayed behind had to exploit every possible resource in an increasingly hostile environment. They carried on hunting game and gathering the fruit and seeds of wild plants. From 2500 BC, people started cultivating selected strains of wild millet.

Home in the sands Nomads living in the zone north of Lake Chad make huge mats from the reeds
growing on the edges of the lake. They use these to construct matting tents, held down by stones.

2500 years ago were erecting vast standing stones, each weighing several tons. In the west, groups of stone circles scattered across the savannah north of the River Gambia date from more recent times; some have been carbon-dated to around AD 750. They may mark the burial mounds of kings and chiefs.

Bronze catfish A weight, probably for fishing.

The realms of Ghana

By the 8th century AD, the empire of Ghana, not to be confused with the modern country of Ghana, was the dominant power in West Africa. Its heartland lay in the southwestern corner of present-day Mali, and its people, the Soninke, controlled the trade routes linking North and Central Africa. The great markets of Ghana – cities such as Aoudaghost on the southern edge of the Sahara – were bustling, cosmopolitan meeting places, where Berber and Arab merchants arrived with their caravans from the north to exchange iron tools, textiles and, above all, salt for the gold and ivory coming from the south. Muslim chroniclers left glowing accounts of the wealth and power of Ghana. Decline set in during the 11th century, when the Almoravids, a confederation of militantly Muslim Berber tribes, started attacking Ghana from the north. They captured Aoudaghost in 1054 and the capital Kumbi in 1076.

By now, Islam, based on the teachings of the prophet Muhammad, and inspired by faith in one God, Allah, was spreading in the region south of the Sahara in the wake of

Nok head A terracotta head from the Nok culture of Nigeria around 1st century BC.

trade and conquest, winning new followers and new empires. From a power base in modern Guinea, the Malinke people established the empire of Mali – again, not to be confused with the modern country of that name. Its founder was a devoutly Muslim chief, Sundiata, who started to expand his territories in the upper Niger region from

around 1230. Like Ghana before it, the great empire of Mali owed its wealth to trade: in slaves, gold and ivory from the south, and in weapons, jewellery and salt from the north. It reached its peak under the emperor Mansa Musa (reigned 1307-32). He became fabulously rich after incorporating the other great trading centres of Gao and Timbuktu (Tombouctou) into his realm.

When Mansa Musa went on pilgrimage to Mecca, he took a retinue of 60 000 attendants and 80 camels laden with more than 2 tons of gold to distribute to the poor along his way. The effect of this largesse is said to have destabilised the gold markets of Cairo and other cities for years.

The Songhai Empire

Gao stands strategically on the banks of the Niger, where the River Tilemsi flows into it from the north. Its people, the Songhai, were already rich from the trans-Saharan trade when Mansa Musa made

Stone circle Megaliths found in Senegal and The Gambia probably mark the burial places of important chiefs. The practice continued until around AD 1000.

An audience with the emperor of Ghana

'He is enthroned in a pavilion around which stand ten horses caparisoned with cloth of gold. Behind him are ten pages carrying shields and swords with golden pommels, and, to his right, are the sons of the princes of his empire, splendidly clothed and their hair woven with gold.'
From the 11th-century Muslim chronicler, El Bakri

High chief *An early French depiction shows a Bamileke chief from Cameroon. Ranked on either side are his living attendants, and behind them are the spirits of his ancestors.*

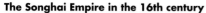
The Songhai Empire in the 16th century

Royal mausoleum *At Gao in Mali, the tomb of the Songhai Empire's Askia rulers doubles as a minaret.*

them part of his empire in the 14th century. A hundred years later, they had regained their independence, and from the 1460s a new ruler, Sonni 'Ali, carved out an empire of his own.

Under his former commander-in-chief, Muhammad Askia, who seized the throne after the death of Sonni 'Ali, the Songhai Empire stretched in an immense 1550 mile (2500 km) swathe from the Atlantic to Lake Chad. Under the patronage of the devout and generous Muhammad Askia, its second city, Timbuktu, became one of the Islamic world's foremost centres of learning. In the second half of the 16th century, however, the wealth of the Songhai realms attracted the envy of Sultan Ahmad al-Mansur of Morocco, who launched an invasion in 1591.

The Moroccan forces included European mercenaries, armed with an alarming new weapon – the musket. In the traditional African way, the Songhai army, armed only with bows, arrows and spears, started the battle by stampeding a herd of cattle against the enemy. The tactic backfired. At the terrifying sound of the firearms, the cattle turned tail and plunged panic-stricken through the Songhai's own ranks. Within a few months of this defeat at the battle of Tindibi, both Timbuktu and Gao had fallen to the Moroccan invaders.

In the region around Lake Chad, the kingdom of Kanem had prospered since the 9th century AD from a three-cornered trade linking North Africa, the Nile valley and Central Africa. In the 14th century, pressure from the nomadic Bulala people forced Kanem's ruling dynasty, the Sef, to withdraw to Bornu, west of Lake Chad. Here, they continued to prosper and by the 16th century they had regained their former realms in Kanem. The Sef king, or *mai*, claimed to be of divine descent. Such was his holiness that he held audiences behind a curtain and was believed not to need to eat. Any unauthorised person unfortunate enough to see the camels delivering food to the palace was put to death. The dynasty did prove to be long-lived: the last Sef king died in 1846, bringing to an end nearly 1000 years of rule by the same family.

Holy wars

In the middle Sénégal valley, the Tukulor people converted to Islam in the 11th century, but it was not until the mid 19th century that they started to build an empire. Under the religious leader al-Hajj 'Umar, they launched a series of holy wars against neighbouring peoples to bring them into the Muslim fold. They were successful at first, but then came up against the might of France's African empire; by the century's end they had been brought under French

Timbuktu's house of worship *The Djingareiber mosque in Timbuktu is a characteristic example of the banco (mudbrick) architecture of the region. It has been reconstructed several times.*

rule. By contrast, the ancient feudal kingdom of Mossi survives to this day, within the modern state of Burkina. Its paramount ruler, the *morho naba* ('big lord'), still holds court in the capital, Ouagadougou, though with largely ceremonial powers.

Priest-king *A brass statue from the 15th century shows a king of the Yoruba's holy city of Ife. He is holding and wearing the emblems of his office, both kingly and priestly.*

The heads of Benin

When the Dutch merchant David van Nyandael visited the *oba* (king) of Benin near the start of the 18th century, he was impressed by '11 human heads moulded in copper, each surmounted with an elephant's tusk'. Nearly 200 years later, the heads, the possession of which was believed to confer legitimacy on the oba, were dispersed. In 1897, the reigning *oba* refused British troops permission to pass through his realms – which lay in south-western Nigeria, not the modern state of Benin. In retaliation, the British mounted a raid against him, burnt his capital and seized many of its treasures, including the heads, which ended up scattered among the world's great museums.

All the king's men *Brass reliefs depicting armed warriors decorated the palace of the oba, or king, of Benin. They were among many treasures scattered after British troops set fire to his capital, Benin City, in 1897.*

Lost wax sculptures

Gold, copper and leaded brass are all used to make sculptures in the lost-wax (or *cire-perdue*) process. The craftsman first makes a wax model of the sculpture. Having attached small wax rods to the model – for metal to be poured into the mould at a later stage in the process – he lays several coats of fine clay over the wax to create a cast or mould of the model. He heats the mould until the wax runs away through the holes formed by the wax rods. Then he pours molten metal into the resulting cavity. When the metal has cooled and solidified, he breaks open the clay mould, and uncovers an exact replica in metal of the original wax model.

Brass chameleon *Ashanti and Baule craftsmen from the Guinea Coast used gold and brass to make small symbolic representations of different animals.*

Traditional African religions are animist: natural phenomena and things, animate and inanimate, are believed to possess spirits. Among the Mossi, Islam and animism have blended. Friday may be the Muslim holy day, but on Friday morning the *morho naba* carries out rituals connected with the royal fetishes, magical objects believed to contain the essence of kingly authority.

Cities of the coast

On the forested plains of the Guinea Coast, unlike the open savannah grasslands of the interior, conditions did not favour the emergence of large empires. Tsetse fly made it difficult to raise livestock or to make use of horses – vital to maintaining control of extensive realms. As a result, power tended to gather in the hands of a few chiefdoms, established at key points where trade routes crossed.

In southern Nigeria, the Yoruba people established a cluster of city-states in the region west of the point where the River Benue flows into the Niger – places such as Oyo and Owo, still important cities. They lie along the line where the upland savannah meets the rain forests of the coastal plain, and grew rich from the trade between the two zones. Each city was independent, but they had a common cultural and religious centre in the city of Ife, supposedly founded by a son of the Yoruba god Oduduwa. This had become an important kingdom by the 11th century AD.

The craftsmen of these cities included superb sculptors, who created realistic terracotta heads and objects in cast metal, usually copper or leaded brass (an alloy of copper, zinc and lead), using the *cire-perdue* (lost-wax) process.

Yams, cultivated in Nigeria since the 4th millennium BC, were the region's staple food, a reliable crop which nourished the highest population density in Africa. Population pressure was one factor in a succession of westward migrations along the Guinea Coast, resulting in the foundation of new kingdoms. The Dahomey kingdom in modern Benin and the Ashanti kingdom in modern Ghana were both established in this way in the 17th century. Around 1750, a breakaway Ashanti group, now known as the Baule, settled in Ivory Coast, under their queen Awura Pokou.

In Central Africa, the kingdom of Kongo dominated the region around the mouth of the River Congo, when Portuguese navigators and traders arrived there in the 15th century. Its capital until the 18th century was M'banza-Kongo in north-western Angola. Inland, the interconnected Luba and Lunda peoples established kingdoms

Parallel powers Traditional chiefs and kings still have an important part to play in the lives of their peoples. The king of Dahomey in present-day Benin holds audiences wearing a silver nose-guard to protect him from harmful influences.

which controlled the region's copper mines and minted small copper crosses, used as currency. They also controlled much of the trade across the interior of the continent, ultimately linking Portuguese trading posts in the west with Arab ones along the Indian Ocean coast. The authority of their king or paramount chief was based on *bulopwe*, a sacred force believed to be inherited from the founder of the dynasty and symbolised by the stool on which he sat on ceremonial occasions.

The age of navigators

It was a Portuguese prince who first promoted the systematic European exploration of Africa. From 1420, Prince Henry the Navigator – younger son of John I of Portugal and his English queen, Philippa of Lancaster – sponsored a series of expeditions down the continent's Atlantic coast.

The kingdom of Kongo in the 15th century

Regal splendour The king of the Ashanti in modern Ghana holds an audience, surrounded by objects in gold and silver. These symbolise his authority and are believed to ward off evil spirits.

Salt trade Salt was a key commodity traded on the trans-Saharan routes. Here, in the Fachi oasis in the Ténéré desert of Niger, briny water in depressions is poured into jars, then left to evaporate in the sun. The blocks of poor-quality salt left behind are carried south and fed to the livestock of the Sahel.

European society developing a taste for sugar, the Portuguese and their trade rivals soon realised that they had access to a new and highly lucrative commodity – human beings, to be shipped across the Atlantic to work as plantation slaves in the Americas.

New trade routes

The European bases along the Guinea Coast seriously disrupted the traditional trans-Saharan trade routes. Camel caravans were an easy prey for bandits, and had to contend with the rigours of one of the most hostile environments on Earth. A single European ship, meanwhile, could carry as much merchandise as several hundred camels. The textiles, iron tools and other goods that had once reached sub-Saharan Africa only on camelback now also arrived, often more economically, by sea. The result was a shift in the balance of power within West and Central Africa. The coastal peoples, controlling the trade with Europe, prospered; the old empires of the savannahs, their monopolies broken, declined.

Religion mingled curiously with profit as a motive for exploration. Ships and crews were blessed before they set sail. Priests and missionaries worked alongside the merchants, bringing the gospel to 'unenlightened' peoples. And all the while, the 'triangular trade' was expanding. Ships set out from European ports, laden with arms, metal goods, cheap jewellery, textiles and

By 1445 Portuguese navigators had reached the mouth of the River Sénégal; by 1448, they had established a trading post on Arguin island, off the coast of modern Mauritania. The expeditions continued after Prince Henry's death in 1460. In 1483, Diogo Cão reached the mouth of the Congo – so vast that at first he took it for an arm of the Indian Ocean. Five years later, Bartolomeu Dias reached the Cape of Good Hope. In 1497-9, Vasco da Gama made his epic journey to India and back around the bottom of Africa. For the first time, Europeans had access by sea to the valuable spice trade of Asia.

The early Portuguese navigators traded for gold and ivory along what came to be known as the Gold Coast of modern Ghana. Here, in 1471, they built another

fortified trading post, El Mina (the mine), on the edges of a lagoon. But the supplies of gold were not limitless, and competition from other Europeans, establishing their own posts along the Guinea Coast, became intense. Following Columbus's 'discovery' of the New World, and with

Mother, child and slave In a trading post off the coast of Senegal, a local 'lady of quality' has her own African slave.

The triangular trade

NORTH AMERICA
EUROPE
Atlantic Ocean
AFRICA
areas supplying slaves
West Indies
Equator
SOUTH AMERICA

↝ slaves   ↝ tropical produce   ↝ trinkets, weapons etc.

Fighting for abolition

By the end of the 18th century, many Europeans had come to see slavery as a monstrous evil. In Britain, the slave trade was denounced by the philanthropist and MP William Wilberforce. He and a number of his friends were the driving force behind the Society for Effecting the Abolition of the Slave Trade, founded in 1787. Two years later France, in the early stages of its Revolution, abolished slavery, though Napoleon, under pressure from disgruntled colonials, reimposed it in 1794. Britain abolished the trade in 1807, and slavery itself in 1834. France abolished slavery in 1848. Communities were also established where freed slaves could be repatriated to Africa. These included Freetown in Sierra Leone (founded in 1787), Liberia (1822) and Libreville in Gabon (1849). In Brazil, slavery continued until 1888. In Zanzibar and certain Saharan societies, it continued into the 20th century.

liquor. In West Africa, these were exchanged for slaves, who were then packed into the ships' holds for the infamous 'middle passage' across the Atlantic. The same vessels returned home to Europe, bearing the produce of the New World: sugar, molasses, cocoa, coffee, cotton and indigo.

The scale of the European slave trade was unprecedented. Arab merchants had carried

The victims of slavery

The European slave trade lasted roughly 350 years, from the late 15th century to the early 19th century. During that time, an estimated 25 million slaves may have been transported across the Atlantic. But the effects extended wider than that. For every one of the 25 million, another five people were probably indirect victims of the slave trade, as a result, for example, of the wars it helped to foment. These led to famine and death. Nor do the 25 million include slaves who died of disease during the 'middle passage' or committed suicide. The Arab slave trade probably counted as many victims, but spread over about 12 centuries, rather than three and a half.

The pioneers Statues of Portuguese navigators gaze out over a terrace on São Tomé, first settled by the Portuguese in the 16th century.

on a thriving commerce in slaves from sub-Saharan Africa for more than a thousand years. The slaves were used as household servants or agricultural workers, tending palm groves. Within sub-Saharan Africa itself, war captives were traditionally enslaved, though their offspring had some hope of freedom. Female slaves might become wives of their masters, males serve in the armies of their new lords. Both were soon integrated into the nation that had

enslaved them. In the American and West Indian colonies, by contrast, the slaves formed a permanently servile stratum of the population.

The European trade destabilised Africa for centuries. It encouraged war, because a successful war meant prisoners, which meant slaves, who could be traded with the Europeans for commodities such as firearms.

Scientific interest

By the end of the 18th century, a growing abolitionist movement in Europe went hand in hand with a vigorous interest in Africa from a geographical and cultural point of view. In 1788, a group of British scientists and men of letters, including the president of the Royal Society, Sir Joseph Banks, founded the African Association in London to sponsor exploration of the interior of the continent.

Until then the European presence in Africa had mostly been confined to its fringes – trading stations built at the mouths of rivers or on the edges of coastal lagoons. Rivers offered the most viable routes into the heart of the continent, but

Armed outpost Gorée island, with a strategic position off Dakar in Senegal, belonged in turn to the Portuguese, the Dutch, the British and the French. Each of its different occupants added to its defences, hoping to fend off interlopers from the rival European powers.

in many cases, notably the Congo, rapids and cataracts made them unnavigable for long stretches. Nonetheless, the Europeans started establishing bases farther and farther inland. The British had a station at Pisania (now Karantaba), 200 miles (320 km) up the River Gambia. In 1818, the French established one at Bakel, 340 miles (550 km) up the Sénégal.

European exploration of the interior began as the 18th century ended. In 1795-6, the African Association sponsored the Scottish surgeon Mungo Park, to explore the course of the Niger. Making his way up the Gambia, he cut across the upper basin of the Sénégal and reached Ségou on the Niger before a lack of supplies forced him to turn back. During a second expedition in 1805-6, he travelled downstream as far as the Bussa rapids in western Nigeria, where he drowned during an attack by Africans.

Two decades later, in 1827-8, a Frenchman, René Caillié, set out from Senegal disguised as an Arab traveller, and spent two weeks in the Muslim holy city of Timbuktu. He was followed in the 1850s by the German Heinrich Barth, dedicated to a more scientific quest than his French predecessor. He spent six months in Timbuktu as well as exploring and mapping large parts of the Lake Chad region and the upper reaches of the River Benue.

The scramble for Africa

The man who more than anyone else opened up the Congo basin to the outside world was the Welsh-born journalist Henry Morton Stanley. Famous for his rescue of

Soldiers of the cross *An engraving from the 1890s shows Catholic missionaries opposing the use of forced labour in Central Africa.*

the Scottish missionary and explorer, David Livingstone, Stanley spent five years from 1879 in the Congo, building roads and launching steamers on the river's navigable reaches. His sponsor was the Belgian king, Leopold II, who as the head of a consortium of investors effectively annexed the so-called Congo Free State as his own private estate. It marked the start of a headlong 'scramble for Africa' by the industrial powers of Europe, each determined to claim its share of the continent's markets and rich resources of raw materials.

In 1884-5, the German chancellor Otto von Bismarck called an international conference in Berlin to try to bring some order to the process. In their eagerness to share out what Leopold II described as the 'African cake', the great powers often drew ruler-straight lines on the map that took no account of African realities. The frontier between Togo and the Gold Coast, for

Holy city *French explorer René Caillié made discreet sketches of Timbuktu during his stay there in 1828 disguised as an Arab traveller.*

instance, split the Ewé people assunder; and the Hausa, Fulani, Yoruba and Ibo, all with their own proud traditions, were combined whether they wished it or not, along with some 250 smaller ethnic groups, in what became the nation of Nigeria.

France extended its control over most of the savannah region and Ivory Coast, Britain over the Gold Coast (modern Ghana) and Nigeria. In many cases, the local peoples resisted, but the Europeans were skilful at exploiting intertribal enmities. For the most part, colonial governments

Mystic conqueror *An engraving shows the 19th-century Muslim mystic and founder of the Tukulor Empire, al-Hajj 'Umar.*

White explorer *Stanley painted by the modern Congolese artist Tshibumba Kanda Matulu.*

provided an administration, but left the commercial exploitation of a territory to business enterprises. Colonies were supposed to be self-financing. Abuses were almost inevitable. In 1904, the Irish-born British consul to the Congo, Roger Casement (later executed for his part in the Irish Easter uprising of 1916), published an account of atrocities in the Congo Free

The rise of African nationalism

African soldiers returning home at the end of the Second World War had remarkable tales to tell – of how their colonial masters had been defeated and humiliated in Europe and East Asia. Their stories gave credibility to a growing nationalist movement, led by figures such as Kwame Nkrumah in the Gold Coast (now Ghana), Nnamdi Azikiwe in Nigeria, Léopold Sédar Senghor in Senegal, Félix Houphouët-Boigny in Ivory Coast, Ahmed Sékou Touré in Guinea and Modibo Keita in French Sudan (Mali). At first these men, most of them European-educated, called only for greater self-government in their territories. All of them, however, went on to become presidents or prime ministers of independent nations.

State against people forced to work in the lucrative rubber industry. An international outcry obliged Leopold II to hand over his personal powers in the territory to the Belgian government. Between 1921 and 1934, the building of the Congo-Océan railway, linking Brazzaville in the French Congo with the coast, cost the lives of an estimated 15 000 to 20 000 forced labourers.

Winds of change

The First World War had emphasised the importance to the European powers of their African colonies – both strategically and as a source of food and raw materials. In the

Muslim empires

The 19th century was a time of upheaval in West Africa. In a climate where old balances of power had been upset, partly by the slave trade, militantly Islamic realms established themselves in the region. The first was founded by the reformer Usman dan Fodio in north-west Nigeria. Between 1804 and 1809, Usman, from the Fulani people, launched a series of jihads, or holy wars, to bring other local peoples, mostly Hausa, under his version of Islamic rule. In the mid-century, another Muslim cleric, al-Hajj 'Umar, from the Tukulor people, established an Islamic realm, stretching from the uplands of Guinea as far as Timbuktu. The Tukulor Empire fell to the French in the 1890s. In the 1880s, a third Muslim leader, Samory Touré, built up a kingdom in the Upper Volta region. He was defeated and captured by the French in 1898.

Piling them high Groundnuts (or peanuts) are one of Senegal's chief exports.

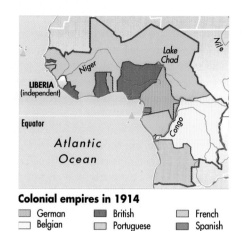

Colonial empires in 1914
German, Belgian, British, Portuguese, French, Spanish

aftermath of the Second World War, however, the sums seemed to add up another way. Private investors continued to profit from the colonies, but governments found the administrative burden increasingly expensive. As early as 1946, in a speech in Brazzaville, Charles de Gaulle promised to take account of African aspirations to greater self-government. By 1960, in a speech in Cape Town, the British prime minister, Harold Macmillan, was talking about the 'wind of change' sweeping across Africa. At government level, at least, European investment in Africa was no longer yielding viable returns.

When the British-ruled Gold Coast gained its independence in 1957, the whole continent looked on with eager interest. The newly independent nation – which called itself Ghana, after the medieval empire of that name – was the first European territory in black Africa to shake off the colonial yoke. Just two years earlier, a conference of Asian and African states and territories, held in the Indonesian city of Bandung,

State visit De Gaulle and President Senghor of Senegal reviewing a guard of honour in Paris, 1961.

and representing more than half the world's population, had condemned 'colonialism in all of its manifestations'. Nationalism was on the rise around the globe, and the grip of the European empires was loosening.

Winning independence

In Africa, the movement towards independence was gathering momentum, though the legacy of past injustices and tensions was soon to become all too obvious. Independence was followed by bloody upheavals in countries including Nigeria, the Democratic Republic of Congo (Congo-Kinshasa, formerly Zaire) and Angola.

France, the biggest colonial power in Central and West Africa, made a cautious concession towards nationalist aspirations in 1956, when it extended the franchise and the right to self-government within its territories. Two years later, President Charles de Gaulle put the issue to a referendum: the African territories would be granted full internal self-government as co-members with metropolitan France of a French Community. All voted yes, except Guinea, where the nationalist leader Ahmed Sékou Touré declared: 'We prefer poverty in liberty to wealth in slavery.' In the event he turned out to deliver oppression, along with poverty.

The nationalist tide was running too strongly for limited self-government. By 1960, the colonies of French West and Equatorial Africa had achieved full independence. Many were aware of the danger that colonial rule would simply be replaced by fragmentation – a region split into small countries, often pulling against one another, rather than together. But when Senegal and French Sudan (present-day Mali) experimented with a federation, it fell apart in a year.

British Nigeria achieved independence as a strongly centralised federation in 1960. The most populous state in Africa, Nigeria was torn by rivalries between the predominantly Muslim north and the Christian and animist south, and among its three major ethnic groups: the Ibo in the south, the Yoruba in the south-west and the Hausa-Fulani in the north. When three eastern states tried to secede as an independent republic of Biafra in 1967, they sparked a three-year civil war in which a million people lost their lives. In the end, the Biafrans were forced to surrender and reintegrated into the federation.

Celebrating freedom *Independence day festivities – here being celebrated in Congo-Brazzaville – are a time for affirming national unity in face of the ethnic and other forces that threaten to shatter it.*

One-party rule

Inevitably, the founding president or prime minister in most countries was the same figure who had led the nation to independence. In these circumstances, it was natural, though not necessarily healthy for democracy, for a 'cult of personality' to gather around him. Kwame Nkrumah, first president of Ghana, liked to be known as 'the Redeemer'. Strong leaders, impatient with opposition, were tempted to impose one-party rule, and to gaol opposition leaders. In many of the newly independent states, economic problems were added to ethnic tensions because, as a legacy from colonial

days, they depended on single crops whose value see-sawed on world markets.

Often the enforcers of one-party rule were the military. In 1963, President Sylvanus Olympio of Togo was ousted in the region's first coup d'état. Many others followed. Not even the grand old man of pan-African politics, the 'Redeemer' Nkrumah of Ghana, was immune. He fell in 1966. By the mid 1970s, army officers had taken over in most countries in West and Central

Africa's false start

Between 1880 and 1914, Britain, France, Germany, Belgium and Portugal parcelled out between themselves vast territories in Africa. The colonial era lasted for only a handful of decades, but as well as re-drawing the map of Africa, the European powers warped its economic development. They plundered their colonies' mineral wealth and required them to produce cash crops for export, rather than food for home consumption. Africa is still paying the price.

Civil war *In Sierra Leone, the weakness of the central government led to the emergence of armed militias commanded by rival warlords.*

Boy soldiers *Civilians are the first victims in any war. Village teenagers are recruited into the militias of the warlords, instructed in the use of arms and then sent off to fight rival groups.*

Africa. Perhaps the most grandiose of personality cults was that of Jean-Bedel Bokassa of the Central African Republic. He seized power in 1965, proclaimed himself president for life in 1972, then like a would-be Napoleon crowned himself emperor of a Central African Empire in 1977 – before being ousted with the help of French troops two years later.

In Ghana, Flight Lieutenant Jerry Rawlings was representative of a younger generation of officers, often impatient with what they saw as the corruption and betrayed ideals of their elders. He staged a coup to oust his country's existing military regime in 1979, handed over to a civilian president,

seized power again in 1981, was elected president in multiparty elections in 1992 and finally stood down in 2000.

New hopes for democracy

By the 1990s, multiparty democracy had begun to make headway. In Benin, the military ruler President Mathieu Kérékou had adopted Marxism-Leninism as the state ideology. In 1989, however, with the Iron Curtain collapsing in Europe, he initiated reforms which ended in multiparty elections two years later.

The end of the Cold War, and of Soviet involvement in Africa, meant that the Western powers also had less incentive to remain

involved. Aid levels tumbled. The most visible Western presence now came from multinationals, often exploiting as single-mindedly as the colonial powers of old the continent's riches in oil, diamonds, metal ores, timber, cotton, cocoa and other crops. Political and economic mismanagement combined with ethnic and religious rivalries resulted in bloody civil wars: in Liberia from 1989, in Sierra Leone from 1991, in Congo (Congo-Brazzaville) between 1993 and 1999 and in Congo-Kinshasa from 1996. In Angola, riven by civil war since before its independence from Portugal in 1975, the death of the rebel leader Jonas Savimbi in February 2002 raised cautious hopes of peace.

African Union

In July 2002, African leaders met in Durban, South Africa, for the last meeting of an old organisation and the first of a new one. The old body was the Organisation of African Unity (OAU), set up in 1963 when Africa was still casting off colonialism. The new body is the African Union (AU). Whereas the OAU came to be seen as little more than a 'dictators' club', the AU is designed to address the needs of a new age. It is envisaged that it will eventually have a peacekeeping force, a central court of justice and a central bank.

The vote race *In Ivory Coast, coup leader Robert Gueï sought to legitimise his seizure of power in 1999 with a presidential election in October 2000. He was obliged to flee, however, after allegations that he and his followers had rigged the poll.*

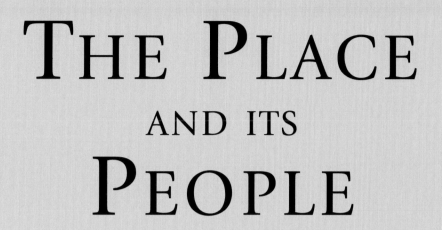

THE PLACE
AND ITS
PEOPLE

Sub-Saharan Africa offers a spectacular
variety of peoples, landscapes and wildlife.
Its people range from the desert-wandering, blue-
veiled Tuaregs to the pygmies of the rain forest,
with their superb tracking skills; its buildings
from simple mud huts to gleaming skyscrapers.
Its wildlife is the stuff of marvels, though many
species are now threatened with extinction.
It is only natural that Africans should seek to
exploit the resources of their land, but they know
they have to walk a fine line, so as not to exhaust
all that makes that land unique.

CHAPTER 1

JEWELS OF NATURE

Everything about the climate and landscape of Central and West Africa seems to be marked by excess.
The sun can be pitiless, drying out soil and crops. Rain can come in torrents, leaving behind a waterlogged land. In the north, the dunes of the Sahara stretch out in strangely geometric patterns that suggest some stark, elemental force is in control. It is a threatening force, too, for the desert is advancing implacably into the cultivable land to its south. The mountains that rise above the Guinea Coast are symbols of durability – their oldest rocks date from more than 2.5 billion years ago. Sandy beaches and mangrove swamps lie along the coast, while inland are endless savannahs and the perpetual heat and humidity of the rain forests. The Niger and the Congo, snaking across the region, add the thrilling spectacle of their falls and rapids.

In the far north of Cameroon, marshy plains are backed by the peaks of the Mandara Mountains.

The call of the desert

The southern Sahara stretches in a great swathe from Mauritania and Mali in the west, across the Republic of Niger and into Chad. And it is on the move: every year it creeps a little farther south, encroaching on the Sahel, a region of semidesert and dry grassland.

Doum palm

There is something inescapably humbling about the desert. If you are going to survive there, say the Sahara's nomadic inhabitants, you have to recognise that it is bigger than you are: you have to place yourself in God's hands. If God wills – *Insh'Allah* – the rains will fall. Fortunately, a little rain is quite enough to make the desert bloom. With just 0.8 in (20 mm) of precipitation, the dormant *acheb* pastures, consisting of a mass of different bushes and grasses, spring into hectic activity, cramming an entire life cycle, from germination to the sowing of their seeds, into the space of two or three weeks.

Salt routes across the Sahara

Also if God wills, the fodder for the camels of the Azalai salt-caravan will last the 370 mile (600 km) trek between Agadez in central Niger and the salt-producing oasis of Bilma. Salt is one of the precious commodities of the region, once traded for gold and slaves. The Azalai caravans are a relic of huge camel trains, numbering as many as 20 000 animals, that crisscrossed the Sahara until the early 1900s. They plied between saltworks at places such as Bilma in Niger and Taoudenni in Mali and the great trading centres at Agadez and Timbuktu.

For humans, oases are the key to survival in the unremittingly dry landscape of the Sahara, where temperatures rise above an oven-like 55°C (130°F) at the hottest time of the year and sink below freezing point on winter nights. In these green havens, set among the surrounding wastes, irrigation systems built up over generations nourish stately groves of date palms, in whose shade crops of fruits, vegetables and even cereals grow.

Plants and animals have made numerous adaptations in their battle for survival. Desert mammals include jerboas, gerbils, mole rats, hyraxes, hares and sand foxes or fennecs. Mostly, they are nocturnal, taking shelter from the heat of the day in deep burrows. Mostly, too, they are small; one of the largest is the addax antelope, standing 40 in (1 m) high at the shoulder. Yet the Sahara was not always so daunting. Rock paintings, notably

Ancient survivor *The dwarf crocodiles of Ennedi have hung on for 4000 years, isolated from their remote Nile ancestors.*

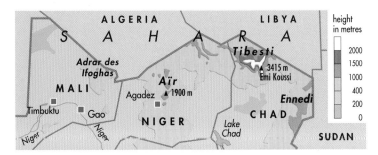

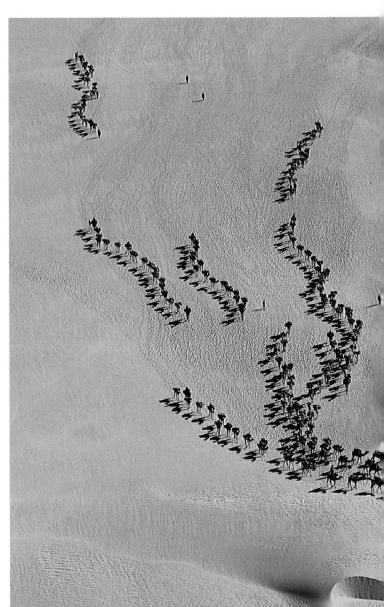

On the salt route *Camels carrying millet trek across the dunes of the Ténéré desert (right). In Bilma, the millet will be exchanged for salt.*

in the Tassili n'Ajjer, a high plateau in the central Sahara, depict animals that now exist farther south, including giraffes, elephants, rhinoceroses and cheetahs. Even now, a surprising range of creatures survives in the massifs of Niger and Chad. Among them are wild barbary sheep or *aoudad* in the Aïr and Tibesti mountains. The Tibesti massif also has the Sahara's highest peak – an extinct volcano, Emi Koussi, rising to 11 204 ft (3415 m) above sea level, and snow-capped in winter.

Olive, or anubis, baboon

Sandstone wonders in the Ennedi

In the Ennedi massif on the eastern edge of Chad, near its border with Sudan, erosion has carved the sandstone into a fantasy of shapes – natural arches, jagged needles prodding skywards, steeply rising peaks and deep, canyon-like wadis. The arch of Aloba is one of the wonders of the Sahara, 130 ft (40 m) wide and more than 260 ft (80 m) high. Spreading out in a deeply gouged wadi is the Guelta d'Archei, a small permanent lake fed by underground springs.

Among the many animals living here, the most surprising perhaps are a small group of about ten dwarf crocodiles, the descendants of Nile crocodiles which thousands of years ago made their way from Lake Chad, up the Bah el-Ghazal (now a dry wadi) as far as Archei. Feeding on the fish of the lake and wadis, they are living reminders of the era when the Sahara was green. Nor are they the only such survivors. In 1997, a French expedition discovered another group in Nohi wadi.

Rock, scrub and sand *The ruins of a fortified village rise from the desolate wastes of the Djado plateau in the far north of the Niger.*

Addax antelope

Peoples of the desert

Two traditionally nomadic peoples – and rivals – stand as symbolic figures of the Sahara: the Tuareg and the Tubu. The Tuareg (above), often known as the 'Blue Men', from the indigo-dyed veils the men wrap around their faces, are Berber-speaking herdsmen. They wander over a vast region of the Sahara which includes parts of Libya, Algeria, Mali and Niger. The Tubu, also herders, speak a Nilo-Saharan language, one of a small family of tongues spoken only in Central and North Africa. They are concentrated in the Aïr, Tibesti and Ennedi massifs and in the Fezzan region of south-western Libya.

Both peoples raise camels and goats in the Sahara, while groups living farther south in the Sahel also raise zebu cattle. Their societies are organised on feudal lines, with a warrior nobility at the top and labourers (formerly slaves) at the bottom of the social ladder. Despite their nomadic traditions, a growing number of both the Tuareg and Tubu peoples are being channelled into a more settled life.

35

The mighty Congo

From its headwaters in the south-east, the River Congo forms a huge arc across equatorial Africa, then heads for the Atlantic in a tumble of rapids and falls. Its navigable inland waterways are the key that opens the heart of the continent, a world of their own where convoys of river steamers and barges are like floating towns.

River train *River steamers and barges on the Congo are colourful splashes of life in a scene dominated by water and forest.*

Africa's high interior plateau rises like a gigantic citadel, its ramparts pierced by a handful of rivers such as the Congo (or Zaire). Not even these provide an easy point of entry. Portuguese navigators in the 16th century travelled up the Congo for about 100 miles (160 km), until they reached the series of rapids and cataracts now known as the Livingstone Falls. These guard the entrance to Malebo Pool, a lake-like expanse, 17 miles (28 km) long and 15 miles (24 km) wide, dominated by the island of Mbamou. Kinshasa, capital of the Democratic Republic of the Congo (formerly Zaire), stands on the lake's shore; Brazzaville, capital of Congo, lies across the water, on the south-western shore.

River of mystery

The Congo kept its secrets until 1877, when the British journalist Henry Morton Stanley made an epic journey down the river, starting near its sources on its main headstream, the Lualaba. It is the second-longest river in Africa, after the Nile – 2900 miles (4700 km) from headwaters to ocean. By volume of water, it is the world's second-largest, after the Amazon. The rate of flow at its mouth is 1.45 million cu ft (41 000 m³) per second. The weight of water flowing into the Atlantic has gouged out a 500 mile (800 km) submarine canyon in the ocean floor.

Legend and mystery cling to the Congo, and the words of Joseph Conrad, in his novel *The Heart of Darkness* (1902), still ring true: 'Going up that river was like travelling back to the earliest beginnings of the world, when vegetation rioted on the earth and the big trees were kings. An empty stream, a great silence, an impenetrable forest.' This forest is home to Pygmy

On the waterfront *Villages cluster to the banks of the river highway. Here, in Katanga province, it is called the Lualaba river.*

Rapid catches *Fishermen of the Wagenia people net their prey in traps, which they hang from fishing platforms.*

A harvest of fish

The waters of the Congo and its tributaries are rich in fish. Perched on precarious-looking platforms, riverside villagers net huge quantities of the tasty *capitaine* fish (also known as *mbuta* or Nile perch) and large catfish, which they send off to the markets in Brazzaville or Kinshasa. The town of Mossaka in Congo-Brazzaville is a famous fishing centre. Every year in May or June, when the water level drops, its fisherfolk set out for a season of intensive activity. Catches are best when the water is low, so they fish solidly until October when the rains come in the headwater regions, and water levels rise again.

peoples. Its wealth lies in its minerals and in its timber, the great trunks that are felled, then floated downstream to sawmills. The most precious woods include gaboon (used for veneers), ebony, mahogany and a mahogany-like wood known as sapele. The Pygmies call the sapele the exchange tree: traditionally they leave gifts at the foot of a sapele for their neighbours, the 'big people'.

Life on the river

From Malebo Pool upriver as far as Kisangani, the Congo is navigable. Above Kisangani are the Boyoma Falls; upstream again is the gorge known as the Gates of Hell. On navigable stretches, the Congo and its tributaries form a vital highway, where river steamers tug flotillas of double-decker barges behind them. The largest carry 5000 people on journeys that may last days – or weeks. Dugout canoes will launch out from the banks, and noisy but good-natured haggling will break out as soap, sugar, fish hooks or medicines change hands. Sometimes, passengers will put ashore for markets selling edible caterpillars along with the meat of crocodiles, monkeys, parakeets and antelopes. They may stay on for a drink or two before heading back to the quay to wait for the next convoy heading in the right direction.

The Congo basin

White water
The Livingstone Falls (below) are a series of 32 rapids and cataracts that stretch out over about 220 miles (350 km) of the Congo river.

The little people of the forest

There are about ten different Pygmy peoples scattered across equatorial Africa, making up a total population of perhaps 200 000. The include the Bayaka of the Central African Republic, the Efe and Mbuti of Congo-Kinshasa and the Babinga of Congo-Brazzaville.

Adult Pygmies are anything between 4 ft (1.2 m) and 5 ft (1.5 m) tall. Traditionally, they have been hunter-gatherers, who live from the riches of the rain forest – fruit, fish and game.

They have always maintained links with the wider world, often performing special roles in neighbouring societies. The Twa Pygmies of the south-eastern highlands of the Congo basin, for example, traditionally acted as musicians for the local chiefs – the close harmonies of Pygmy singers can be powerfully moving.

In recent years, however, the Pygmies' traditional way of life has been disrupted by the logging industry. Outsiders coming into the forests to work for logging companies kill the game the Pygmies rely on for food. Many Pygmies themselves have gone to work in the logging camps and villages where a number have fallen prey to blights such as disease and alcoholism.

Forest home   *A Pygmy camp with shelters of leaves and branches.*

Mountains, peaks and plateaus

The granite and sandstone ranges looming above the Guinea Coast are among the oldest on Earth, their peaks levelled to rugged plateaus by thousands of years of erosion. Rising from the dunes of the Sahara, the imposing Hoggar, Aïr and Tibesti massifs are of volcanic origin. Farther south, West Africa's highest peak, Mont Cameroun, is a still-active volcano, bringing fertility as well as danger to the surrounding plain when it erupts.

Nature's tower *A column of volcanic rock looms above the surrounding uplands in the Mandara Mountains along the border of northern Cameroon and Nigeria.*

In times of trouble, Saharan peoples have often sought refuge behind the volcanic ramparts of northern Chad's Tibesti massif. Tibesti's peaks include the Sahara's highest mountain, Emi Koussi (11 204 ft/3415 m above sea level), and together with steep-sided valleys and deep gorges present a formidable barrier to any would-be invader. Their volcanic origins are clear in the huge crater, 3¾ miles (6 km) across, that crowns Pic Toussidé (10 712 ft/3265 m).

To the west, the Hoggar and Tassili n'Ajjer massifs in southern Algeria and the Aïr massif in northern Niger are linked to Tibesti by a region of uplands. The upper slopes of the Aïr massif's deep valleys, known as *koris*, bake under the desert sun, but in the valley bottoms reeds grow, along with wild fig and olive trees, some of them thousands of years old. Their long root systems enable them to tap water lying several feet underground.

Watershed for West Africa

The Fouta Djallon is a rugged sandstone block in central Guinea. Along with the granite Guinea Highlands, sweeping down like a tail to the south-east and including parts of Sierra Leone, Liberia and Ivory Coast, it forms the watershed for this part of West Africa: the

rivers rising on its flanks include the headwaters of the Niger and Sénégal rivers. The climate here is influenced by the *harmattan*, a hot, dry wind blowing from the north-east, chiefly in winter, picking up dust from the Sahara and carrying it far out into the Atlantic. Its effect in the Fouta Djallon is to produce a long, dry winter season, lasting from December through to June, followed by torrential monsoon-style rains. Savannah grasslands, dotted with clumps of trees, cover the uplands of the Fouta Djallon. To the south-east,

Fulani cattle-herders

Communities of the Fulani (or Peul) people live right across West Africa, from Senegal in the west to Chad in the east. They are herders by tradition, raising cattle for dairy produce rather than meat. Two of the largest groups are in the Fouta Djallon and the Adamaoua plateau of Cameroon. But their original homeland was the Fouta Toro region of Senegal, from where in the late 18th and early 19th centuries, their leaders launched a series of holy wars to convert neighbouring peoples to Islam. One group established a state in the Fouta Djallon, with the town of Timbo as its capital. Another, under Usman dan Fodio, set up an empire in northern Nigeria. Usman's son Adama took the holy war to the region of Cameroon that now bears his name – Adamaoua. Although many have settled in towns and cities, considerable numbers remain true to their traditions. They move around with their herds, carrying with them large huts as homes. Some have adopted a more settled, rural life, which includes growing crops as well as herding cattle.

Red earth *In the Gorges de Diosso, in Congo (Brazzaville), rain has carved the red laterite soil, rich in iron and aluminium oxide, into natural buttresses.*

the Guinea Highlands have a much longer rainy season, especially on their seaward-facing slopes, where it may last ten months. Some places regularly record more than 118 in (3 m) of rainfall in a year.

Cloud of death

The Mandara Mountains are a volcanic range, marking the border between northern Cameroon and Nigeria. Farther south, the volcanic peaks of the Adamaoua highlands dominate central Cameroon. These are dotted with crater lakes, most notoriously Lake Nyos, where in August 1986 a huge bubble of compressed carbon dioxide burst from the depths of the lake, letting loose a poisonous cloud that killed more than 1500 people. On the coast, Mont Cameroun (13 451 ft/4100 m) rises from the plain, a volcanic outcrop twinned across a narrow sea strait by the 9869 ft (3008 m) cone of Pico de Santa Isabel on the island of Bioko.

Over the edge *Waterfalls abound along the edges of Guinea's Fouta Djallon and neighbouring Guinea Highlands. Many of West Africa's rivers have their headwaters in these uplands.*

A forest of spires *In Congo (Brazzaville)'s Mayombé massif, thousands of years of erosion have left natural pinnacles capped with hard slabs of quartzite.*

39

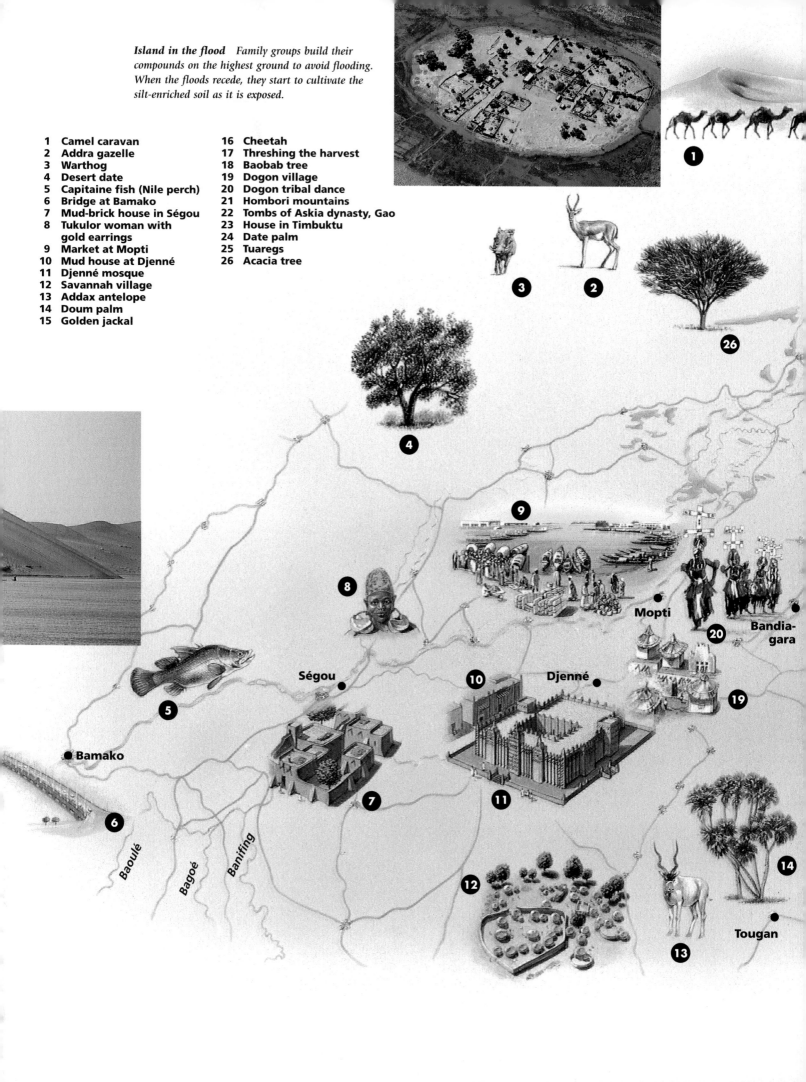

Island in the flood Family groups build their compounds on the highest ground to avoid flooding. When the floods recede, they start to cultivate the silt-enriched soil as it is exposed.

1 Camel caravan
2 Addra gazelle
3 Warthog
4 Desert date
5 Capitaine fish (Nile perch)
6 Bridge at Bamako
7 Mud-brick house in Ségou
8 Tukulor woman with gold earrings
9 Market at Mopti
10 Mud house at Djenné
11 Djenné mosque
12 Savannah village
13 Addax antelope
14 Doum palm
15 Golden jackal
16 Cheetah
17 Threshing the harvest
18 Baobab tree
19 Dogon village
20 Dogon tribal dance
21 Hombori mountains
22 Tombs of Askia dynasty, Gao
23 House in Timbuktu
24 Date palm
25 Tuaregs
26 Acacia tree

Bamako

Ségou

Mopti

Djenné

Bandia-gara

Tougan

Baoulé

Bagoé

Banifing

The Niger: an African highway

Rising in the highlands of Guinea and flowing for 2590 miles (4200 km) to the sea, the Niger curves in a great arc through all the main types of landscape to be encountered in West Africa. It tumbles off the savage sandstone heights that gave it birth, then flows through open savannah grassland into a vast inland delta, a labyrinth of lakes, swamps, sluggish streams and backwaters where much of its initial force is sapped by the heat of the sun and lost to evaporation. It remains a mighty river, however, a great provider to those who live along its banks, and an important highway of trade today, as it was in the days when it was a key factor in the growth of the ancient civilisations of Timbuktu and Gao. It turns to the south-east near Timbuktu, watering the sands of the Sahara before reaching more savannah. In central Nigeria, the Niger is joined by the last of its great tributaries, the Benue. It continues its majestic progress through a belt of rain forest towards the mud flats and mangrove swamps of its sea delta, the Mouths of the Niger, in the Gulf of Guinea

Downstream is for washing   Villagers who live along the Niger go downstream from their homes to wash themselves and their clothes, but move upstream to draw water for drinking.

Among the dunes   In its northernmost arc, east of Timbuktu, the Niger flows through the desert. A handful of settlements perch on its banks, using irrigation to create tiny oases.

Hedgehog mosque   The mosque at Djenné is the largest mudbrick building in the world. Having fallen into disrepair, it was rebuilt in 1905, using the original design dating from the 11th century. The bristling wooden beams make life easier for workers when they renew the mud rendering after the rainy season each year.

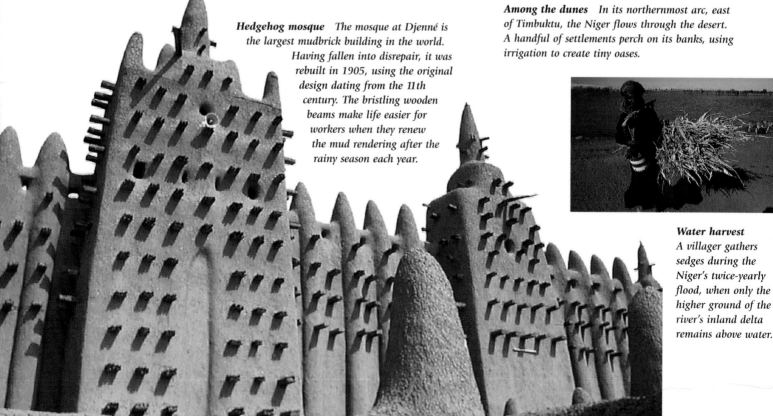

Water harvest
A villager gathers sedges during the Niger's twice-yearly flood, when only the higher ground of the river's inland delta remains above water.

The River Niger

1 Life-giving grain
The well-irrigated plains around the inland delta are the region's granary, growing millet, sorghum and beans. The millet is winnowed, pounded and made into a nourishing porridge.

2 Delta livestock
Fulani herdsmen bring their flocks to market in the Macina region of Mali. The rich soils of the inland delta provide excellent grazing.

3 Tomb of mud 'Banco' construction, using mud bricks with a mud rendering, is a traditional building method in the middle Niger valley – as here in the tombs of the 16th-century Askia dynasty at Gao.

4 The water run
The river is a lifeline for the communities scattered along its banks, providing water for household use and irrigation for the fields.

5 River trader For at least 1000 years, the Sorko people have used their large dugout canoes to fish and carry goods along the stretches of the Niger south of Gao.

6 The broom sellers
A market trader shelters from the sun under his umbrella. Traditional crafts thrive in the communities of the middle Niger valley – from weaving and dyeing to broom making.

7 Sand dune and paddy field Farmers plant rice when the river is in flood. In this region of stark contrasts, desert and cultivated land often lie side by side.

Shells for money For centuries, cowrie shells, originating in the Indian Ocean, were used as currency across large parts of sub-Saharan Africa. They were used in small country markets well into the 20th century.

Wedding day The dry season brings a pause in the farming year, a time for festivals and celebrations, as at this marriage between two Songhai families from Timbuktu.

By canoe to market In Africa, rivers unite people, rather than divide them. They are the highways by which the people living on their banks get around. These men are heading for the large livestock market at Ayorou in the Republic of Niger.

Water market Canoes made from hollowed-out tree trunks are moored alongside the market at Mopti. Their shallow draught makes them ideal for the smooth, often shallow waters of the inland delta. Such canoes carry huge quantities of goods, from salt to millet to baskets of dried fish.

The Niger

Sénégal · Timbuktu · **MALI** · Gao · **NIGER** · Niger · Mopti · Niamey · Bamako · Bani · Djenné · **GUINEA** · Lake Chad · **NIGERIA** · Niger · Benue · **CAMEROON** · Niger Delta · Gulf of Guinea

Outside the walls A young Fulani woman sits outside a mosque built in the traditional pinnacled, 'banco' (mudbrick) style of Mali.

Life on the edge By the height of the dry season, the grasses of the Sahel have withered almost entirely. Sheep and goats are kept in round pens made from acacia thorn branches.

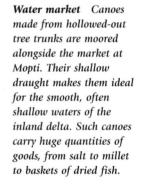

Mud bath *Children wallow in floodwater. The Niger has two floods: the 'black flood' of clear water from January to March, and the 'white flood' of silt-laden water from April to September.*

Gourma-Rharous

Gao

● **Timbuktu**

● **Douentza**

Punting through *A villager poles his dugout pirogue canoe through a bank of sedges in the inland delta. These grass-like plants are used as animal fodder and for thatch.*

Beaches, creeks and mangroves along the coast

It is not by chance that most of the capital cities of West Africa lie on or near the coast. In past centuries, rivers seemed to be the best means of penetrating into the interior, but voyagers soon found their way barred by rapids and waterfalls, as the rivers tumbled off the high plateau. But the coastal plains were fertile, the sea provided fish, and, through trade, a village could grow into a kingdom.

A mountain barrier rises from the plains of the Guinea Coast, the area that stretches for 3000 miles (4800 km) from Africa's westernmost top to the mouth of the Congo. Clouds sweeping in off the ocean are forced upward and dump their loads of rain before they reach the high interior. The coasts of Liberia, Sierra Leone and Guinea bear the brunt of weather systems coming in off the Atlantic. Portuguese explorers gave Sierra Leone its name, meaning 'lion mountain', because of the frequency and lion-like violence of the storms buffeting this shore.

Mangroves: a rich environment in decline

From the mouth of the Congo as far north as the Sénégal, mangrove forests cluster round the mouths of rivers and along the edges of lagoons with high salt content. Creating fantastical mazes with their stilt-like prop roots, the mangroves are home to a range of wildlife from small rodents to large, juicy prawns, oysters and mussels. These provide rich pickings for local communities, whose hunters propel their dugout canoes along narrow waterways, often entirely overhung with vegetation. These leafy vaults, forming the aisles of some great natural cathedral, are home to countless birds. Worldwide, mangroves are in decline, as a result partly of pollution, partly of rising sea levels, due to global warming.

High seas, tranquil lagoons

River-borne mud and sand have been deposited along the coast in the form of deltas and sandbars. The deltas, most notably the vast region known as the Mouths of the Niger, have been colonised by a tangled fringe of mangroves. The sandbars, stretched out by the warm, west-flowing Guinea Current, face the stormy Atlantic on one side, but shelter tranquil lagoons on the landward side. For the most part, the coast-dwellers build their villages on the quieter shores facing the lagoons.

Many of the coastal communities profited from the arrival of European merchants from the late 15th century, establishing themselves as middlemen in the trade with the interior. Some

Sheltered waters *An islet in Ivory Coast's Ébrié Lagoon is a reminder of how Abidjan, now a busy port, looked when it was a village.*

The ten volcanic islands and five islets that make up the Cape Verde archipelago lie 370 miles (600 km) into the Atlantic. Situated in latitudes where the skies are cloudless most days of the year, they suffer severely from droughts. Those of the 18th and 19th centuries caused around 100 000 deaths. The capital, Praia, gets just 10 in (260 mm) of rain in a good year. During the brief rainy season, springs can flow in the hills, allowing the valley bottoms to be irrigated. Elsewhere, the islands' black slopes are bare and eroded.

Beach landing   *A fishing boat comes in to land in Sierra Leone. In the background, Africa's interior plateau rises sharply from the shore.*

of the lagoons had openings onto the sea. The European arrivals dredged and widened them, and built their trading posts close by. In this way today's bustling ports, such as Abidjan in Ivory Coast and Lagos in Nigeria, were born. In more recent times, artificial deep-water harbours have been created at places such as Lomé in Togo.

Islands in the gulf

Until the 16th century, the islands of São Tomé and Príncipe and Bioko were uninhabited dots in the sea. For the Portuguese, however, they provided handy staging posts and collection points for slaves. The newcomers also established sugar plantations where they set slaves to work. Today's islanders are the mixed-race descendants of African slaves and Portuguese slave-traders. Nowadays, they grow cocoa and coffee in the black soil of the islands' steep volcanic slopes.

Casting their nets   *Boys join their fathers in gathering the catch in Togo, while others run into the heavy Atlantic surf to cast their nets.*

Life on the open grasslands

Sandwiched between the Sahara to the north and the equatorial rain forests to the south, the savannah grasslands of West Africa stretch in a wide band from Senegal to the Central African Republic. They are home to a rich array of animal-life – including herds of grazers and browsers and the predators that feed off them.

The serval *The wild cat of the savannah.*

Bordering the Sahara along its southern fringe, the Sahel (from the Arabic for 'shore' or 'edge') is a transition zone – from desert, to semidesert, to savannah. The savannah here is at its driest, a sea of short grasses, dotted with occasional thorn bushes, mostly acacias. During the rainy season, which barely lasts two months, the grasses spring up green and fresh; for most of the rest of the year, they are a bleached yellow-brown.

Food from the savannah

Farther south, the rains last longer. There are more trees and shrubs, which often grow in clumps. Many have edible fruits and roots, making a significant contribution to the diet of the local people. They include the stately baobab tree, undisputed king of savannah vegetation, bearing nutritious fruit as well as offering shade under its wide-spreading branches. The nut-like fruit of the shea tree is a source of vegetable oil, known as shea butter. In places, gallery forest forms, dense thickets of trees and shrubs growing along the edges of watercourses. The short grasses of the northern zone give way to species such as elephant grass, which grow up to 15 ft (4.5 m) tall in some cases. In savannah woodlands, the tree cover becomes thicker still, forming a light canopy that blends, almost imperceptibly, with the rain forest.

Parched though they are for much of the year, the grasses of the savannah provide sustenance for huge numbers of grazing animals, from buffalo to warthog, hartebeest to bushbuck. Elephant and giraffe browse the foliage of trees and shrubs. Prowling in the background are the predators – lion, leopard, cheetah and their smaller relative, the serval, a long-legged cat that feeds off birds, rodents and lizards. Packs of spotted hyena hunt prey for themselves and scavenge on the prey of others. Jackals are mostly scavengers.

In the savannah, humans and wild animals have always lived at close quarters. During their festivals, the farming peoples of the savannah perform ritual dances wearing animal masks, as if acknowledging that the animals were there before them.

Termite towers The brown ramparts of termite mounds rise among the savannah grasses.

Putting goodness back into the soil

The termites of the savannah help to regenerate soil that has lost key nutrients, often through years of intensive crop-growing. Termites feed on the cellulose of grasses and dead wood. In this way, they break down – sometimes with the help of a special fungus – the nutrients locked up in the cellulose.

These are returned to the soil in the termites' waste, as well as through the huge mounds – some up to 16$\frac{1}{2}$ ft (5 m) high – which they build out of earth mixed with their saliva.

Parched land *Grainstores dot the dry grasslands near Tahoua in the Republic of Niger, on the edge of the Sahara.*

In the depths of the rain forest

Mini hippo *No bigger than a wild boar, the pygmy hippo is a nocturnal creature living in the forests of Liberia and Guinea. Though a good swimmer, it is less fond of wallowing than its larger cousins.*

The swathe of rain forest, stretching from Gabon on the coast east into the Congo basin, is the second-largest in the world, after the rain forests of the Amazon. Although under constant pressure from logging companies and land-hungry farmers, it survives as an unparalleled reserve of biodiversity.

No habitat on Earth offers a more ideal set of conditions for life and pulsating growth than the rain forest. It is like a gigantic greenhouse, with heat and humidity present all year. The sun's rays strike the forest canopy with such intensity that they encourage a prolific growth of fruit and foliage, providing food for monkeys and brilliantly coloured birds.

A world of twilight

The trees, many of them hardwoods much coveted by loggers, are massive. Trunks can be up to 30 ft (9 m) in diameter, and the treetops rise 165 ft (50 m) above the forest floor. Monkeys and chimpanzees spend much of their time in the topmost levels. The middle layers become a twilit world, for the canopy filters out much of the light. This is the realm of the potto and Senegalese bush baby, both of them primitive primates. They share it with leopards, well hidden among the light-dappled leaves, and pythons, sliding from branch to branch. The forest floor provides little nourishment other than insects, roots and fallen leaves, fruit and nuts. But there is enough food for small creatures such as the royal antelope, no bigger than a hare.

With a guide who knows how to 'read' the forest, the evidence of animal activity is all around: the spoor (tracks) of a bush or red river pig, the burrow of an aardvark, the tramplings of forest elephants. If you follow these to a clearing, you may, with luck, catch a family of lowland gorillas at play.

Riverside village Many rain forest dwellers establish their villages along the banks of the Congo and its tributaries.

The sacred groves of Benin

Rain forest once spread all along the Guinea Coast. Nowadays, it survives only in pockets. In many cases, these owe their survival to the *voduns* – the word for 'god' or 'spirit' in the language of the Fon people of Benin, and from which our word 'voodoo' is derived. The forest people have set aside special groves as homes for the *voduns*, marking them by hanging a garland of palm leaves from a trunk, or by placing a pot of food at the foot of a tree. They go there to perform initiation ceremonies and other sacred rites. Strictly speaking, hunting and logging are not allowed in these forests. Nowadays, however, even the great irokos, most sacred of all the forest trees, are felled, though offerings may be left as a gesture to try to appease the *voduns*.

Wild Africa's national parks and reserves

A century ago, there were an estimated 2 million chimpanzees in the whole of Africa. Today, poaching and habitat loss have reduced that number to 150 000. That, in two sentences, is the heart of the case for conservation. The world has an irreplaceable treasure in the national parks and reserves of Central and West Africa, havens of the lion, leopard, elephant, gorilla, crocodile and a vast array of birds.

The tragic death of American naturalist Dian Fossey on Boxing Day, 1985, brought worldwide attention to the plight of the mountain gorillas of the Virunga range in Central Africa. Fossey had made it her life's work to study the magnificent apes, increasingly endangered by the fatal combination of poaching, habitat loss and endemic warfare and unrest in the region. In the end, it was poachers, seeking out gorilla flesh for the highly profitable bushmeat trade, who murdered her. Bush meat, the meat of gorillas, chimpanzees and other wild animals, is widely sold in African markets; local conservationists and their supporters abroad see the trade as the biggest single threat to the survival of several species.

Primates in danger

Fossey's death helped to make the mountain gorillas famous, but their cousins, the western lowland gorillas of the western Congo basin, are no less threatened. One problem here is the fate of

Grey and green *Low clouds hang over the rain forest of southern Cameroon.*

orphaned gorillas: these creatures' parents were shot for the bushmeat trade, and the offspring, too small to be any good for meat, are sold as pets. Well-patrolled reserves at Lesio-Louna in Congo (Brazzaville) and Mpassa in Gabon have special facilities for reintroducing them into the wild. There was another orphanage at Brazzaville zoo, but in 1997 when a civil war was being fought out in the streets of the capital, troops of the French Foreign Legion set up an air bridge to evacuate the gorillas to a sanctuary near the

Endangered primate *The drill lives mostly at ground level.*

Saving the drill

The drill, a large monkey which once lived widely in the rain forests of Nigeria and Cameroon, is now one of the most endangered primates in the world. It was brought to this pass by a combination of habitat loss and the bush-meat trade. Paradoxically, local tribal traditions forbid people to eat the flesh of large monkeys. But for workers brought in from outside by logging companies, poaching monkey flesh for sale in city markets is a good way of supplementing their wages. At the same time, the drill is particularly vulnerable to the felling of huge swathes of forest. A troupe of 200 individuals, with females that give birth just once every two years, needs a large, uninterrupted territory in order to survive. In the Afi River Forest Reserve in the south-eastern mountains of Nigeria, the Drill Rehabilitation and Breeding Center has a programme of reintroducing the animals to the wild. But it faces an uphill task in a country where the rain forest is disappearing at the rate of 3 per cent a year. According to the Nigeria Conservation Programme, three-quarters of the forest that existed just 20 years ago has now gone. Nigeria has been slow to preserve this heritage: less than 8 per cent of its forests are protected.

Giant in hiding *A mountain gorilla in the Virungas National Park.*

Sable antelope

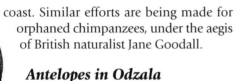

coast. Similar efforts are being made for orphaned chimpanzees, under the aegis of British naturalist Jane Goodall.

Antelopes in Odzala

Sanctuaries, reserves and national parks are vital to the survival of Africa's wildlife heritage. In northern Congo (Brazzaville), Odzala National Park encompasses 5250 sq miles (13 600 km²) of rain forest. Clearings in the forest, known as 'salines', offer a compelling display of animals, drawn there by rich accumulations of essential mineral salts in the soil.

Visitors arriving in the early morning may catch glimpses of forest buffalo and graceful gazelles; of slender duiker antelope, with black foreheads and grey-brown coats; tiny water chevrotain, standing just 12 in (30 cm) high at the shoulder; water-loving sitatunga, with shaggy coats and a white mark on their faces; large but timid bongo antelope, standing 4 ft 3 in (1.3 m) at the shoulder, with magnificent white-striped chestnut coats. Gallery forest, bordering the banks of the Mambili river, is home to

A park on the small scale

National parks are not always vast stretches of savannah, rain forest or river delta. On the outskirts of Ivory Coast's largest city, Abidjan, the Banco National Park covers just 12 sq miles (30 km²), carved out in 1953 around the banks of the Banco river. It is one of the last vestiges of the rain forest that once covered the whole region but was largely felled to make way for coffee, cocoa and palm plantations. Small though it is, the park retains its magic. The sounds of the city give way to bird calls and the rustling of small animals in the undergrowth.

At the water hole *Bongo antelopes in the Central African Republic's Dzangha-Sangha reserve. They are timid creatures, rarely seen in the open.*

Bush pig

51

On the prowl *A rare daytime sighting of the mostly nocturnal leopard.*

two kinds of wild pig, the bush pig and the giant forest hog, while overhead squirrel-sized talapoin monkeys, with special cheek pouches for carrying food as they forage, leap from branch to branch.

The elephants of Waza

In the narrow northernmost finger of Cameroon, near its borders with Nigeria and Chad, Waza National Park covers 620 sq miles (1600 km²) of dry savannah and is home to some of the most abundant and varied wildlife in the whole of Africa.

Darting across the plain when startled are huge herds of Thomson's gazelle, sable antelope, waterbuck and topi antelope. Prowling through the grass are the great feline predators, lions and leopards, and carrion-eating scavengers, such as jackals and hyenas. Birds include ostriches and marabou storks. Above all, Waza National Park has some of the largest surviving herds of the savannah elephant – protected by special police and army patrols. At midday, when the sun's scorching heat brings most other activity to a halt, up to 300 elephants and giraffes gather round the waterhole known as Elephant Pond.

Protecting the wildlife heritage

Governments in the region are increasingly taking steps to preserve their wildlife. Nouabale-Ndoki in Congo (Brazzaville) was established in 1993, and is one of the largest rain-forest parks in Africa, covering nearly 1500 sq miles (4000 km). Three countries – Benin, Burkina and the Republic of Niger – cooperated to create the National Park of the W, so named because it stretches out from a great double bend in the Niger river.

Senegal, with one of West Africa's best-developed tourist industries, has no fewer than six national parks. In the south, near the border with Guinea, Niokolo Koba National Park, with 3470 sq miles (9000 km²) of savannah and gallery forest along the banks of the Gambia river, was declared a UNESCO World Heritage Site in 1981. It shelters significant numbers of the Derby eland, the largest of the antelopes, standing nearly 6 ft (1.8 m) at the shoulder and officially classified as being vulnerable to extinction. In the north, the Djoudj National Bird Sanctuary is another World Heritage Site, covering 62 sq miles (160 km²) of the Sénégal river delta. Many of its species are migrating birds, an estimated 3 million of them, stopping over on their way south to escape the European winter. Other birds that nest here include the white pelican and African spoonbill.

Too precious trunks *Elephants are still being slaughtered for their tusks, in spite of a worldwide ban on the ivory trade, imposed in 1989.*
The leading suppliers of elephant ivory, illegally exported to Asia, are the Central African Republic, Cameroon and Gabon. Below: Hippopotamuses, too, are killed for bush meat, their leather and their teeth, which are another source of ivory.

Malachite kingfisher

Life on the wing: the birds of Africa

From the semi-desert of the Sahel in the north to the rain forests of the south, Central and West Africa are unusually rich in birdlife. Many of it species are resident all year, and unique to Africa, but as winter approaches in colder climates, their numbers are swollen by hordes of migrants from Europe and Asia.

All told, there are around 1300 different species of bird in Central and West Africa – 655 have been recorded in Mali alone. Their colours can be a joy to the eye: iridescent sunbirds, bright yellow weavers, dazzling kingfishers and brilliantly bedaubed parrots and touracos.

Bird armies in the forest

Sometimes, though, their very beauty puts them in danger. The forest people of Central Africa have long hunted parrots for their tail feathers, used in adornment and believed to have magical properties. In the rain forests, large birds seek their food either in the canopy or on the ground: it would be difficult for a parrot, a hornbill

Swooping low *An African fish eagle on the hunt for prey.*

Wading in *Spoonbills prod the waters for food in Senegal's Djoudj National Bird Sanctuary.*

or a touraco to attempt to fly through the tangled barrier of lower branches and lianas. The hornbill uses its huge bill to push through the branches for fruit in the canopy. Its nest is a hole, high in a tree, and after mating it seals in its mate with mud, leaving a gap just wide enough for food to be passed in. She remains a captive, with her eggs and young, for months.

Smaller birds can flit easily through the forest. Sometimes they combine to flush out their insect prey in large mixed-species flocks known as 'bird armies'. Among them are likely to be flycatchers and bee-eaters, twisting agilely to catch insects in flight. The tinier the bird, the more energy it needs in proportion to its size, and the diet of sunbirds is almost pure energy. They peck at the base of flowers with their long, down-curving bills to reach nectar. On

the savannah, birds that are seed eaters can be as big a menace as locusts. The quelea, whose numbers in Africa have been estimated at 100 billion, can devastate harvests of rice, millet, wheat and maize.

As winter comes to northern latitudes, many familiar European birds cross the hostile wastes of the Sahara to seek warmth and food. The nightingale takes its song and the cuckoo takes its call to forests on the edge of the savannah. Migratory birds seem to avoid the rain forests, possibly because the abundance there of food throughout the year means that the bird population is already at its optimum level, and there are no niches for newcomers.

Migrants by the billion

At least 177 species of bird escape the rigours of the European winter by flying south. They add up to 5 billion birds over-wintering in the 7.7 million sq miles (20 million km^2) of sub-Saharan Africa, including 40 million birds of prey (eagles, kites, hawks and vultures), 200 million swifts and 3.3 billion perching birds, including warblers, flycatchers and swallows.

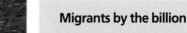

Majestic bearing *Crowned cranes, with their elegant topknots, live mostly near waterholes and lakes.*

53

CHAPTER 2

THE HEART OF AFRICA

Sub-Saharan Africa is a region of 1000 tongues, with as many ethnic groups as there are languages and dialects: the Wolof of Senegal, the Fon of Benin, the Mossi of Burkina, the Ashanti of Ghana, the Mandingo of Liberia. Each group has its own cherished myths, ancestral knowledge and beliefs, passed down from generation to generation. But at the same time as Africans recognise the value of tradition, their continent is going through a period of rapid and unavoidable change. In the villages, women work the fields and raise their families in the way they have done for centuries. In the cities, modern skyscrapers tower over the dwellings of the poor. A sick person may well consult a Western-trained doctor and a traditional healer, both in the same day. Africans have become experts in plaiting together different strands of belief and outlook, in reconciling continuity and change.

Blue represents benign influences, needed by these boys during their initiation rites on reaching puberty.

Collective memories, living traditions

'Every old man who dies is a library that burns,' the Malian diplomat and man of letters Amadou Hampaté Bâ once told a UNESCO audience. The oral tradition, he was pointing out, is irreplaceable. Africa's great treasury of tales and myths, passed down by word of mouth through countless generations, is threatened by growing competition from print and screen.

Family business *The son of a griot is trained in the arts of his future calling.*

The guardian of oral tradition is the *griot*, the bard without whom no West African community is complete. In direct face-to-face contact with his audience, he passes on the group's age-old beliefs and the narratives that enshrine them. Often he accompanies himself on a drum or stringed instrument, the music lending pace and rhythm to a performance that may last a few hours.

Africa still has its traditional chiefs and paramount rulers, whose powers and prestige persist as a shadowy alternative to the authority of the modern state, and every chief has his own personal griot. It is the griot's job to exalt the chief's standing. An expert in genealogy, among other subjects, he can trace the current ruler's ancestry to a heroic forebear whose deeds shed glory on his successors, and recount the great events of the dynasty's history. He also is a master of ceremonies, supervising ritual occasions, making sure that all is done as laid down by tradition.

Master of initiation

At the village level, it is the local griot who organises the initiation rites in the village's sacred wood when children reach adolescence. This is when he explains to them the meaning of the group's various myths – often at night when minds are more suggestible. As in many traditional societies, the myths are a means of teaching the young people about ways of behaving and attitudes of mind that bind the community and embody its ideals.

Old tales, new media *With the advent of radio, television and cassette recorders, the oral tradition has undergone some strange metamorphoses. Many of the ancient tales have been adapted for radio and television.*

Trickster hero

He is not very big and not very strong, but he is usually cleverer than his opponents and so gets the better of them by sheer craftiness. In many parts of West Africa he is a hare, though in some he is a spider – Ananse. With slavery, the tales of his pranks crossed the Atlantic to America, where he became a rabbit – Brer Rabbit. In 1880, an Atlanta-based journalist, Joel Chandler Harris, published a collection of the tales as if told by a wise old ex-slave. *Uncle Remus: His Songs and His Sayings* became a best seller of the day.

Wise men *Whether belonging to a village or the court of a chief, griots such as these two from Mali have a unique status. As well as being storytellers, they are guardians of tradition in a community.*

The continent of many tongues

Making a point Two Senegalese women in conversation.

Africans are natural linguists – they have to be. In a continent where many different communities live side by side and people travel astonishing distances, the variety of languages is immense. Most countries have at least half a dozen languages, some of them used by the majority of the population, others spoken by only a few hundred.

As well as the language of their own particular community, most Africans can speak the languages of neighbouring groups, along with those of the itinerant traders who control much of the continent's internal commerce. Of these languages, the most important by far is Kiswahili, or Swahili, understood and spoken through most of Africa south of the Sahara.

Rival languages

People also have a smattering of languages such as Fulani, spoken by the nomads who pass through their region. Inevitably, many also know the tongue of the former colonial power. Often this has become an official national language, used in the media and in education.

In the savannah regions, where large-scale population movements have been common, a few widely spoken languages

Adult literacy A teacher imparts the skills of reading and writing to a group of women from a rural community in Mali.

tend to prevail, among them Wolof in Senegal, Bambara in Mali, Songhai and Hausa in Niger. In the rain forests, by contrast, communications are difficult, and villages tend to live in isolation from one another. As a result, languages and dialects proliferate – in Gabon around 50 languages have been recorded. The greatest diversity of all occurs in regions that straddle the two zones. An estimated 250 languages are spoken in Cameroon, which lies partly in West Africa, partly in Central Africa.

The diversity of languages is declining, however, and has been for at least a century. In some countries, minority tongues are squeezed out by the official national language, often the one spoken by the dominant political and economic group in the state. Pressure also comes from the former colonial languages, such as English and French, which are more useful on the international stage.

Africa's lingua franca

Originating in Zanzibar, Swahili grew out of contacts between Arab merchants and East African coastal communities. It draws most of its grammar from the Bantu languages of East Africa. Much of its vocabulary comes from Arabic. Later, it borrowed words from Portuguese, English, German and French. When Tanzania gained its independence in 1964, it adopted Swahili as its official language.

Foreign mysteries Pygmy children pore over pictures of badgers and polecats. Passing from an oral tradition to a written one requires textbooks – even if these come from a different culture.

Cities in a hurry

Surprising though it may seem, by the year 2000 there were more people living in Africa's cities than in its villages. And the flow continues, for the cities offer something that has a universal appeal: the hope of a better life. This ambition is just as urgent in the poverty-blighted shantytowns as it is in the smart downtown areas whose borders they lap.

Leading nowhere? *A city avenue comes to an abrupt end in Ivory Coast's purpose-built capital, Yamoussoukro. In many cases, the capital has been shifted to the heart of the country to promote national unity.*

The plane is coming in to land at Abidjan's Port-Bouët airport, and the view from the cabin window shows the abrupt transition where the dark green forest gives way to the open expanse of the Gulf of Guinea, with only the city and the narrow strip of Ébrié Lagoon in between. It seems symbolic of the abrupt contrasts to be found in Abidjan and all African cities. Later, in the taxi ride from airport to city centre, the reality of the sprawling metropolis is inescapable: the heat, the hubbub of horns and voices, the traffic jams and exhaust fumes, an ever-moving sea of humanity.

From village to metropolis

And yet, a little over 100 years ago, Abidjan was a simple fishing village. Until the 1950s, it was still no more than a prosperous town. Now, although the capital was moved to Yamoussoukro in 1983, Abidjan is Ivory Coast's largest city by far, with a population estimated at 3.2 million, and the economic hub of the country.

It owes its spectacular growth to the opening of the Vridi Canal by the French in 1950. This pierced the sandbar that separates

New Africa, old Africa *Skyscrapers dominate Abidjan's Plateau district (above). Standing on the shore of Ébrié Lagoon is the modern St Paul's Cathedral, its tower symbolising arms outstretched in welcome. Right: People and boats crowd the beach of a fishing port near Dakar in Senegal.*

Casual work, urban violence

At first sight, African cities are scenes of joyous disorder, where old skills are constantly being reinvented to meet new needs. Yet behind the colour and bustle are the problems of cities that have grown too big too fast, with too few jobs to go around. In these circumstances, fortune favours the resourceful. Forced to live by their wits, many young men, referred to as *babaye* and *jaguda* or *rarray boys* – names that have taken on a seedy glamour – join criminal gangs, or the militias of warlords.

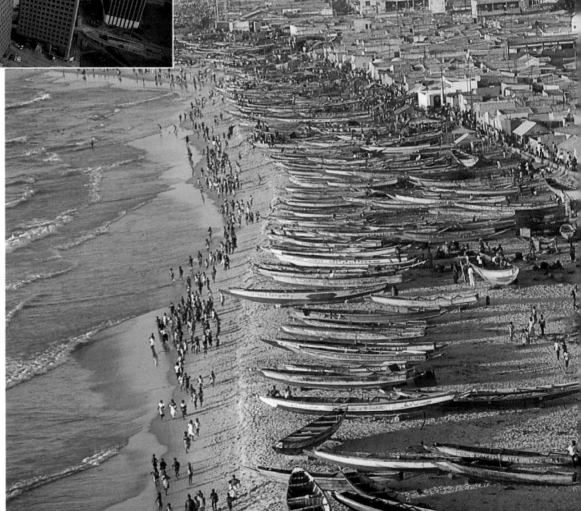

Ébrié Lagoon from the ocean and made it feasible to build a deep-water port, through which cocoa, coffee, bananas, pineapples, timber and manganese are now exported. Abidjan, in common with most of the other big cities of West Africa, was developed by its colonial rulers with an eye to the exploitation of the interior; railways, roads and port facilities were constructed to this end. The great river ports of Brazzaville and Kinshasa on the Congo's Malebo Pool and a string of seaports – Dakar in Senegal, Conakry in Guinea, Accra in Ghana, Lagos in Nigeria and Libreville in Gabon – were the result. In the process, prosperity vanished from the older commercial centres, whether it had been based on the trans-Saharan routes, as in Gao, or on the slave trade, as along the Cape Coast in Ghana.

Red Star Square *The Place de l'Étoile Rouge in Benin's largest city, Cotonou, reflects the country's Marxist-Leninist past as the so-called African Cuba.*

The cities' new elites

The ports were built to meet European needs, and many distortions imposed by these needs still prevail. Most are the economic capitals of their countries, even if they are no longer the political ones. Yet in a strange way they turn their backs on their countries – none of them lies near the geographical heart of its modern state. At the same time, their layouts reflect the divisions that existed between white officials and managers who lived in spacious bungalows, preferably on high ground to receive the benefit of cooling breezes, and black workers, who sweltered in overcrowded low-lying slums.

Nowadays, glass and concrete towers soar skywards among the old government buildings of colonial times. And in the old residential areas, the villas of the new ruling class mingle with sumptuous hotels, such as Abidjan's watering hole for the wealthy, the Hôtel Ivoire, which dominates the smart Cocody district. The shantytowns, meanwhile, continue their own relentless expansion, in Abidjan as elsewhere.

Rural exodus

In Africa, the exodus from village to city started between the wars, then speeded up as the colonies achieved their independence. It began as a flow of single men seeking jobs, but later whole families joined in. The result was a loosening of ties with village communities and a gradual erosion of age-old solidarities.

Nor is this the only price to be paid for the headlong expansion of cities. In many, crime on the streets has become a serious problem. It is a matter of major concern in Dakar, the capital of Senegal and home of a quarter of the country's population. Dakar has just under 2.1 million inhabitants, but its problems are dwarfed when compared with those of cities such as Kinshasa, which has around 5 million inhabitants, or with Lagos, pulsating home of more than 10 million.

Capital transfer

When President Felix Houphouët-Boigny of Ivory Coast chose a central location for his new capital, he picked his own birthplace, the village of Yamoussoukro. Inaugurated in 1983, the brand-new city was equipped with imposing avenues, lined with smart hotels and grand government buildings. Above all, it has the Basilica of Our Lady of Peace, consecrated by Pope John Paul II in 1990. It is one of the largest religious buildings in the world, capable of holding 7000 people sitting down and with 80 000 sq ft (7400 m²) of stained glass windows.

Basilica of Our Lady of Peace

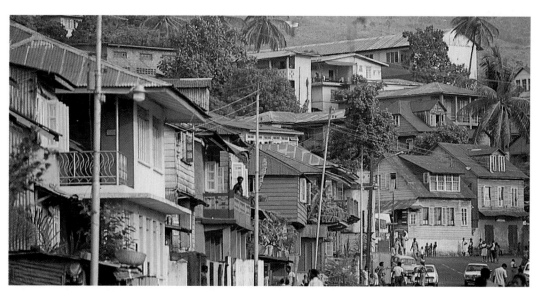

Colonial charm *Wooden buildings with corrugated iron roofs survive in the older trading ports, such as Freetown in Sierra Leone. But with overcrowding and a lack of funds to restore them, they are fast disappearing.*

59

Life on the streets

In Africa, cities tend to combine two different worlds. There is the city of the main thoroughfares, lined with skyscrapers and high-rise office blocks. Then there is the other city, the city of the thronging back streets, whose key points are the bus station and market, the cheap restaurants and night clubs.

The 'official' city is usually the product of colonial planning. It has its administrative district and its business district, its residential areas, with smart villas set in shady gardens, and its 'African' areas, all neatly demarcated . . . except that is not how the bulk of its citizens see it. For them, life spills out – from inside the home or shop onto the streets. People are constantly toing and froing through the city's sectors, selling and buying, telling jokes or exchanging the latest gossip on street corners, going to work, returning from it.

In this version of the city, the working day begins in the small hours. Even before the day has dawned, the multitudes of stall-holders are moving to their pitches at airports and bus stations, in markets and on the pavements. By the time the sun has risen, they have laid out a brightly coloured carpet of fruits and vegetables, sweets and drinks, plastic sandals and cooking utensils. Above them loom the office buildings, where the middle classes are by now arriving for work.

In Abidjan the juxtaposition of the two worlds is most vivid in the Treichville and Plateau districts, lying on either side of a branch of Ébrié Lagoon and linked by a bridge. Treichville's central market is one of the largest in West Africa; Le Plateau is the business district. In Gabon's capital, Libreville, the Nkembo district is home to one of the city's busiest markets as well as to one of its most distinctive places of worship, the Church of St Michel, covered with mosaics and wood carvings of biblical scenes.

The bustle of the market

Every city district has its own local market, which is as much a place to meet people as to buy or sell. In charge here are the women, from the small traders selling vegetables or a few chunks of meat or fish on a piece of cloth laid out in front of them, to the formidable capitalists known in Togo as *nana Benz* (mama Benz

Pedal power *All loaded up and strapped in, a small trader pedals to his pitch (above). Large rolls of cloth are hoisted through the window of a waiting bus (right), which will leave only when it is packed with people and their goods.*

where English is spoken) – market women whose businesses are so successful that they drive around in a Mercedes Benz or some other luxury car. Around the market are workshops of all kinds. Tailors and dressmakers will take the length of material you have haggled over in the market and turn it, within a few hours, into an item of clothing. Jewellers, and an array of menders and fixers, will take just about any piece of equipment and ingeniously extend its life.

A range of eateries

The variety of places to eat caters for all pockets. At the bottom end of the scale is the woman selling simple meals from a basin on the pavement. These will consist of a grain porridge or fritters, mixed with a little meat or fish, flavoured with a spicy sauce. At the top end are the smart European-style restaurants of the business and residential areas. In between lie a range of eateries, including the establishments known in Senegal as *dibiteries*. Here, you watch as a piece of mutton is cut up (*débité*, in French), then grilled over a charcoal fire. Grilled chicken and kebabs are the speciality of *shawarmas*, Lebanese in origin but common across West Africa.

For eating local food in reasonable comfort, the cheap *maquis* restaurants probably offer the best value. Customers arrive, greet one another, make extensive enquiries about each others' families, then settle down for a meal. These places are a key component in the 'pavement radio' by which news, gossip and rumours are disseminated across the city at astonishing speed.

As night falls, action moves to the outlying districts, where men and women stand in front of their homes chatting and laughing – just as they would do back in the villages where many of them were born. From night clubs, the sound of music spills out onto the streets, where taxis draw up, emptying their loads of revellers, ready for a night's dancing.

A bite to eat Eggs, fish and beans are the fare on offer at a foodstall set up at the side of a busy market.

At the bus station

As dawn breaks, the bus station is already a scene of activity. Buses, minibuses and 'bush taxis' – pick-up trucks adapted to carry people and produce – are drawn up in this, the nerve centre of the city. The urchins and grown men who act as porters are leading the first passengers to their vehicles. There is no need to hurry, though, for there is no rigid timetable at the bus depot. But there are plenty of people to chat to, or you can get yourself a snack from a foodstall or just watch the bustle. In the fullness of time, when everybody is on board, your bus or taxi will lurch into action and the journey begin.

In the market Ibrahim, 'specialist Ghanaian barber', plies his trade among stalls selling pots and pans.

Villages at the heart of Africa

No matter where they live, in a big city or even abroad, for most Africans the village remains their central point of reference. They may have adapted to new societies and built new careers, but the village is always home. And if ever they were tempted to cut the ties, the family in the village would soon remind them of their responsibilities to those left behind.

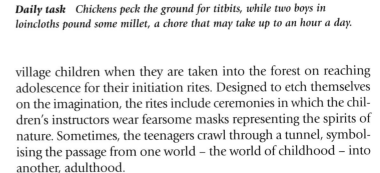

Daily task *Chickens peck the ground for titbits, while two boys in loincloths pound some millet, a chore that may take up to an hour a day.*

Within the village, the key unit is the family compound. Although varying from region to region, a compound usually consists of a group of huts, each belonging to a different branch of the extended family, and surrounded by a wall or fence. The family's livestock is also often kept within the compound.

The skills of survival

The village stands for survival – the need to hang together and accept community disciplines in order to keep going. The enclosure surrounding a family compound is symbolic of this: inside, you are safe; outside lies danger. Essentially, this is what is being drummed into the village children when they are taken into the forest on reaching adolescence for their initiation rites. Designed to etch themselves on the imagination, the rites include ceremonies in which the children's instructors wear fearsome masks representing the spirits of nature. Sometimes, the teenagers crawl through a tunnel, symbolising the passage from one world – the world of childhood – into another, adulthood.

According to widely held beliefs, the earth belongs to god and the spirits. A village elder, chief or wise man – known among some

All-purpose basin *Enamel basins have a multitude of uses: for cooking meals, storing grain or, as here, carrying water from the well.*

Earning the bride price

Economic and social necessity force the young men of the village to seek work in the cities or on cocoa, coffee and timber plantations. A young man betrothed to a village girl has to earn enough to pay the bride price due to her family. And that is just one of the expenses due when, after several years away, he comes home. He must also bring gifts for his own family, and he will be expected to make a contribution to local projects, such as the building of a new mosque or the digging of a new well. Having fulfilled these obligations, he can take his place as a village elder.

Hats of straw *Building styles vary from region to region. Generally, thatch is used for roofs in the savannah zones.*

peoples as 'the father of the earth' – has an especially close relationship with the spirits. He has the authority to distribute land among families or to found a new village. He also knows what offerings are required to ensure the favour of the spirits and the fertility of the land. There is usually a large stone or mound in the centre of the village, where villagers leave offerings of chickens or millet.

Inside the compound

In the savannah, where farmers grow crops and raise livestock, communities are often dispersed. Each family compound is like a mini-village, standing at some distance from the next. Once inside the enclosure, you know you are on private property: the ground is neatly swept. The huts and small granaries that share the compound are constructed in much the same style: round or square walls, made of sun-dried mud and covered by a thatch roof.

In regions where polygamy is the norm, each wife has her

A basket of maize In south-western Burkina, roof terraces are used to sun-dry maize and groundnuts, safe from the reach of rodents and other pests.

own hut within the compound, where she lives with her children. The huts are often arranged in a circle or semicircle. During the day, when not in the fields, the women and children spend their time under thatch awnings, where they sort the grain, prepare the food and look after the babies. Sheep, goats and cattle are kept in a pen within the enclosure. The granaries are raised from the ground to keep them safe from rodents and termites.

In forest regions, villages tend to have a single 'street' lined on either side with huts. These are usually rectangular, with mud walls and corrugated-iron roofs, which provide better shelter than thatch from the torrential downpours of the long rainy season.

Antisocial activities

Craft workers often live apart in their own compounds or villages. This is especially the case if their work could disturb village life or cause annoyance – as with the smoke from a potter's kiln or the hammering in a blacksmith's forge. Koumi, in Burkina, has for generations been a village of iron-workers. It is a warren of banco (dried mud) buildings, where the rooms of one home often communicate directly with those of the next.

Weavers are usually itinerant, wandering from village to village, setting up at the edge of a compound and weaving cloth to order. The arrival of a weaver is a great event in village life: everyone gathers round, watching the work in progress, chatting, hearing the news from the outside world. An alternative place of entertainment is the village drinking shop, where millet beer is stored in earthenware jars. For an outsider, this can be hard to find, except in the forest zones, where bars and primitive restaurants are advertised with brightly painted signs.

Stone and basketware *In mountainous regions, such as large parts of Cameroon, walls are built from stone, rather than banco (dried mud). Sometimes, the straw for the roofs is plaited, as if for basket-making.*

Rites, festivals and celebrations

Birth, puberty, marriage, death – in Africa, where tradition has a rare staying power, all of life's turning points are marked by rites of passage that follow an unchanging pattern. Although taking place within a framework of strict rules, they can be performed with spectacular exuberance. And always to the beat of drums.

People of the chameleon *Lokuta dancers of the Bassari people in Senegal, wearing elaborate masks that will last only for a single season.*

The old woman has died. The news is soon round the village, which lies a few miles outside Garoua in the mountains of northern Cameroon. The people of the village are Fali. The woman is dead, but it is not yet time for her funeral. Instead, the villagers prop up her body in the sitting position, with arms outstretched, then bind it with strips of cloth. They then carry the mummy-like bundle into the mountains, where they deposit it in a hole with a pottery lid to cover its entrance.

Celebrating death

And there the body stays, until a year has passed and it is time for the real funeral. For this event – celebrating the moment when the woman's spirit finally crosses over to join those of her ancestors – people return to the village from far and wide. Having exhumed the body from its resting place in the mountains, they bring it back to the village where they lash the bundle of remains to a tree. Here, it presides over the celebrations. Millet beer; people dance. Later, they take the skull, place it in an earthenware jar and position it, with other similar jars, by the entrance to the village. From now on, the woman's spirit will help to protect the community, so long as the living members keep her well supplied with offerings.

The Fali are animists – what the neighbouring Muslim peoples refer to as Kirdi, or pagans. Similar rituals are found among animist peoples all over Africa. Funerary rites take place months, even years, after people die and commemorate the moment when their spirits reach their final resting place.

Among the Dogon of Mali, this moment is celebrated every five years in the Dama ceremony. It involves dances in which the performers, members of a secret brotherhood, wear special masks, kept for the rest of the time in sacred caves. The most impressive of the masks is the *sirige*, literally 'storeyed house'. It is rectangular, with a long plume-like blade shooting nearly 15 ft (4.5 m) into the air. The mask is said to represent the family home.

The drum beats of initiation

Initiation rites on reaching puberty are no less impressive. Among the Bassari of south-eastern Senegal, the ceremonies begin with the arrival of the Lokuta maskers in the village square. Their faces hooded and haloed with funnel-like masks of basketwork, these fearsome figures perform the 'chameleon dance', in honour

---

The beating heart of Africa

No celebration would be complete without the rhythm of drums. There are as many different beats as there are regions or villages. There is a beat to bring rain, another to bring people into the trance-like state of possession during religious ceremonies. Drumming is traditionally used to pass messages from village to village; it is also a means of communicating with the spirit world. No drummer would start without first seeking the favour of the spirits. Some societies have specialised castes of drummers, in which the finer skills are passed on during initiation. Senegal has a legend that a spirit gave the first drum to mankind, presenting it to a favoured *griot* seer.

Male beauties *Bororo-Fulani youths dressed up and ready to dance.*

The leopard dance Men from a Senufo village in northern Ivory Coast perform their traditional dance of the leopard men.

of Numba, the chameleon god of initiation. Later, the boys awaiting initiation step forward and are beaten with sticks. This marks the first stage of the initiation process; the rest takes place in sacred caves and forests. The dances in the square are paralleled in the drumming that accompanies them. To Western ears, it is percussion, a form of music, albeit a mesmerising one, but to Africans it is a whole language, full of shades of meaning.

Festival finery Straw pompoms and rows of sewn-on cowrie shells, symbols of wealth, are common adornments for festival costumes.

Dancing for a bride

Every year the Bororo-Fulani people of Niger, also known as the Wodaabe, celebrate the end of the rainy season with a festival called the Gerewol. It lasts for six days and nights, during which the young men dance to win themselves a bride. As darkness falls, they disappear into the bushes to take a secret potion believed to make them sexually attractive. The Bororo set great store by male elegance, so the youths wear elaborate headdresses for the dance and make themselves up with red and yellow ochre. At the end of the Gerewol, the girls will make known their choice of husbands – the most beautiful youths and the best dancers.

Flames A fire-eater in Ivory Coast.

Pentecostal prophets, holy Muslim marabouts

Merchants and holy warriors brought Islam to West Africa. Christian missionaries, bringing their faith to the 'dark continent', arrived with the European traders and settlers. The impact of both great religions has been immense, yet neither has succeeded in destroying the region's older beliefs and practices. In the end, Africa has stamped both faiths with its own distinctive mark.

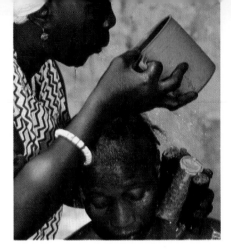

Holy water *Many of Africa's religious traditions use water symbolically to purify and protect the new believer.*

There are a few thousand of them, all dressed in white, packed into the pews of the Synagogue Church of All Nations. They are singing, waiting for the moment when Pastor Temitope Balogun Joshua swings into action. Pastor Joshua is more than just the minister of this Ghanaian Pentecostal church; he is also regarded as a great prophet, famous for his powers of healing. At last he gets up, and starts encouraging people to confess their sins, publicly, allowing him to cast out 'evil spirits'. A woman comes forward. She is possessed, she says, by 'the power of destruction'. 'May the fire purify you,' commands the pastor. The woman collapses, writhing – then quietens down. Finally, she speaks out again: 'I give my life to Jesus.'

The Pentecostal ascendancy

Scenes like this are common across Africa, where the Pentecostal churches and similar Protestant groups have made huge advances. Nigeria now has the second-largest Protestant population in the world, after the United States. For many people, the more conformist Christian churches are simply the religion of their former European masters. Figures such as Pastor Joshua seem to offer answers that are more relevant to their problems.

Sharing some of this appeal are movements such as the Kimbanguist churches, with 4 million adherents in Congo (Brazzaville) and the Democratic Republic of Congo. The Baptist-educated Simon Kimbangu founded his movement in 1921. His miraculous healings and powerful sermons attracted thousands of followers and alarmed the Belgian authorities in Congo, who charged him with sedition. A death sentence was commuted to life imprisonment, and he spent the remaining 30 years of his life in gaol. His movement continued to grow, however, and in 1969 it was admitted into the World Council of Churches. Also in the 1920s, the Liberian-born William Wadé Harris had a similar impact in Liberia and Ivory Coast. The Églises Harristes still thrive in Ivory Coast.

Worshippers in white *Members of a Harriste church in Ivory Coast. The movement was founded by William Harris, who presented himself as the 'prophet of the modern world and spokesman of the Archangel Gabriel'.*

The faith of the brotherhoods

For Islam, the driving force in spreading the faith through West Africa has come from brotherhoods, whose members owe strict allegiance to a marabout (Muslim saint or hermit). One of the greatest of these is the Mouride brotherhood, founded by the Senegalese Amadou Bamba (1850-1927). The Great Mosque at Touba – 106 miles (170 km) east of Dakar – houses his tomb and is the most visited Islamic pilgrimage site in West Africa. Another influential order is the Tijaan (or Tijaniyya) brotherhood, originally founded in North Africa in the late 18th century and inspired by Sufi mysticism. Its chief centres in West Africa are Tivaouane and Kaolack, both in Senegal. Kaolack was the home of the Tijaan marabout Ibrahim Niasse (1900-75), whose influence spread as far east as Nigeria and Chad.

Islam's affinities with African religions are, if anything, stronger than those of Pentecostalism. Above all, although a religion of individual salvation, it keeps the link between the teacher and his disciples, the individual and the group, which is so vital in African societies. In the Islam of West Africa, the marabout takes on a greater importance than in most other parts of the Muslim world. The region has also traditionally offered an extremely tolerant form of Islam, though there are signs that harsher versions of the faith are gaining ground. In October 2000, youths, believed to be Islamic extremists, went on the rampage in the Gambian capital, Banjul, smashing up bars and hotels selling alcohol. And President Yahya Jammeh was said to be threatening to impose Islamic shariah law, though he later denied the reports.

Night trance Bwiti is a secret society among the Fang people of Gabon which blends Christian and traditional African beliefs. Initiates take a hallucinogenic drug obtained from the iboga plant (Tabernanthe iboga) to induce a trance-like state.

Fulani splendour In northern Cameroon, Fulani horsemen celebrate the great festivals of the Islamic calendar by dressing in traditional finery, recalling the days in the early 19th century when they established a Muslim empire in the region.

Sacred remains Touba's Great Mosque houses the tomb of the Senegalese marabout Amadou Bamba.

Ancestral voices: the spirits in everyday life

Among the Dogon people of Mali, he is called Amma. Among the Bobo of Burkina, he is Wuro. The Fang of Gabon, Equatorial Guinea and Cameroon call him Nzame, and for the Yoruba of Nigeria he is Olorun. He is the supreme god or creative force – so distant a figure that mere humans have no access to him. Acting as intermediaries are the countless gods and spirits whose influence is present everywhere.

Every year in August, the Yoruba of south-western Nigeria converge on the town of Oshogbo, drawn to a patch of rain forest lying just outside it – the sacred grove of the river and fertility goddess Oshun. For nine days, the pilgrims celebrate the goddess with feasting and dancing and, on the last day, hold a colourful procession. They would never pay homage to their supreme deity, Olorun, in this way: that remote figure is beyond the reach of human worship. Instead, they honour Oshun along with other deities such as the god of iron, Ogun (often represented as a dog), and the thunder god, Shango. In all, they recognise a hierarchy of 400 gods or spirits known as *orishas*.

Venerated forebears

In many African societies, individual clan or tribal forebears can become gods, and all ancestors are venerated. Beliefs vary, of course, from group to group, but for Africans everywhere, there is never a sharp division between the worlds of the living and the dead. The dead are with us, exercising their influence, beneficial or otherwise. A child is given the name of a dead ancestor to ensure the protection of that ancestor's spirit. Offerings are made to the ancestral spirits of a whole lineage or clan to assure their continuing favour.

Every home has a family altar, tended by the father of the family. Family members leave offerings and sacrifices there to ensure good harvests and harmony among themselves and in the neighbourhood. In some societies, the land itself belongs to the ancestral spirits. The Sara people of Chad see it in terms of marriage: the land is a wife, married to the community, which consists of both the living and the dead. This means that the living cannot make a decision – to start sowing, for example – without first consulting the dead. According to the Sara and to the Serer of Senegal, young people during their initiation rites at puberty are swallowed by the ancestors, to be regurgitated as adults.

Spirit specialists

Certain individuals and groups have a special relationship with the spirit world. These include priests of different kinds, rainmakers, diviners and the members of secret brotherhoods. Through initiation, they have a special knowledge of how to contact the spirits, how to win and keep their favour, how to avoid their reprisals in the form of sickness or bad harvests. Ordinary people in need of advice bring their problems to the priests, hoping for an answer from the spirits.

Among the animist Kirdi peoples of northern Cameroon, diviners use crabs for this purpose. The diviner takes a river crab and places it inside a calabash or jar along with twigs representing the person

Crab that tells the future A diviner from northern Cameroon (above) holds the crab he will use to 'read' the spirits' message. Right: A Fon woman from Benin, dressed for a spirit-possession ritual.

Boyhood to manhood *Bamileke youths from Cameroon, daubed with mud for their initiation rites.*

When god withdrew himself

The Giziga people of Cameroon have a touching explanation of how the creator god, Bumbulvun, came to withdraw himself from mankind. Once upon a time the sky hung close above the earth – so close that nobody could stand upright – and Bumbulvun, the sky god, lived with men and women. He provided generously for people's needs: if you were hungry, you reached up, broke off a bit of sky and ate it. But one day a princess arrived. She did everything the wrong way round. Instead of reaching up for food, she peered down at the ground, looking for seeds. She made herself a pestle and mortar to pound the seeds, but found that when she lifted the mortar up, she was impeded by the sky. So she asked Bumbulvun to pull back a little. Outraged, Bumbulvun withdrew far above to where the sky now is. Since then, humans have walked upright and been eaters of millet. And the god no longer reveals himself. In the old days, he came among people every evening, resolving their disputes. Now, there is no one to do that, and so men go to war.

Women's rites
Women have their own initiation rites in puberty, and their own sisterhoods.

or group consulting him. He then releases the crab and is able to 'read' the spirits' answer in the patterns formed by the twigs.

Spirit possession plays a part in the rites of many peoples, including the Hausa of Niger and Nigeria, the Zerma (or Djerma) of Niger and Mali and the Fon of Benin. During frenzied ceremonies, accompanied by the hypnotic beating of drums, gods or spirits descend on individual worshippers – 'riding them like a horse,' as the saying goes – and inducing an ecstatic, trance-like state in which they utter prophecies.

For the outsider, these are interesting spectacles. But for animist Africans they are a means of coming to terms with life. For them, the spirits ensure the natural order of things. When the order is upset – by the death of a child, say, or a natural disaster, such as drought – their age-old rites and ceremonies offer the hope of restoring the equilibrium.

Health and healing: old ways and new

Although Africa has modern doctors and hospitals, its Western-style health services are stretched. Alongside them, traditional medicine survives, rooted and grounded in age-old African notions of how mind, body and spirit work together to affect health and well-being.

Bush clinic *Nurses in Benin use scales hanging from a tree to weigh a baby.*

In the hospitals, doctors know all about the appropriate drugs and treatments for their patients' diseases. The traditional healers, meanwhile, draw from an ancient lore that has been passed down through generations. They know the secret 'virtues' of plants and are well acquainted with the spirits and their ways. They study a person's soul, and from that deduce what needs to be done.

Mind, body and spirit

For Africa's animists, illness is not necessarily a dysfunction of the body. It may be a sign of a disorder involving both the individual and the group of which he or she is part. The sick person may have transgressed a taboo, flouting the rules that bind the group together and incurred the wrath of the spirits.

The group is particularly important in the case of illness caused by witchcraft. At the simple level, a sorcerer has cast a spell or pronounced a

Keeping evil at bay *Markets sell all kinds of potions and charms for warding off evil.*

curse, usually acting on behalf of an individual or group with a grudge. The remedy against this is a *gri-gri* – a charm or amulet that wards off evil. Much more serious is the case where somebody has become possessed by evil, without being aware of it, and is bringing misfortune on the entire community. This will be proved or disproved by divination or trial by ordeal. The suspected person may be made to swallow poison and vomiting up the poison is a sign of innocence, but succumbing to its effects is a sign of guilt. Those found guilty face the direst of fates – execution (if they have not already perished in the course of the ordeal) or banishment.

Africa's woes

Tuberculosis, sleeping sickness, malaria, elephantiasis – the litany of Africa's endemic diseases tolls on. Malnutrition, tainted water, poverty and warfare, all contribute. On top of these older scourges comes the devastating AIDS epidemic, the biggest cause of death in Africa. It is less serious in Central and West Africa than in southern Africa; even so, in these regions, 15 to 25 per cent of 15 to 49-year-olds are HIV positive. Publicity campaigns try to educate people about the disease. In Cameroon, the authorities issue posters explaining how it is transmitted. In Togo, they promote the benefits of conjugal faithfulness. In Senegal and Ivory Coast, actors go out into the cities and villages with shows to raise awareness. Where governments are unable to respond, non-government organisations have to fill the gap, along with local groups. But one key problem remains: because of expense, the best drugs and treatments are rarely available.

Healing arts *Women learn to be healers and diviners at a school of fetishists at Tenguelan in Ivory Coast.*

Hunting for survival, hunting on safari

In the remote past, hunting was unrestricted in Africa, but today, governments have to balance the preservation of species against the survival of traditional ways of life, as well as to regulate safaris, arranged for the benefit of rich Westerners.

The old way *A Pygmy hunter in the Ituri forest of the Democratic Republic of Congo.*

Among many African peoples, a lion hunt with spears, bows and arrows was a key part of the initiation rites when boys reached puberty. Hunting is still an important activity for village men, and a profitable one – so-called bush meat, which unfortunately often includes the meat of species in danger of extinction, fetches good prices in city markets.

By bow and arrow

In some places village hunters still use their traditional weapons of poisoned arrows and nets, and they often hunt with packs of dogs. Men dig camouflaged pits and set traps in paths used by the animals they are hunting. The pygmies use a kind of crossbow for hunting monkeys. Guns, by contrast, are rare. Where village hunters do have guns, they are usually hand-made by local craftsmen, rather than factory-made.

Because of the difficulty of preserving the meat, hunters rarely stray too far from their village. Nonetheless, trips may last a few days, the hunters sleeping in the forest by night. In this case, they smoke the meat to preserve it. The most common prey are monkeys, antelopes, wild pigs, porcupines and birds of various kinds. Occasionally, hunters may bag a lion, leopard or other big cat. Elephants, too, are sometimes hunted. Although illegal, the trade in their tusks for ivory is lucrative. Elephant flesh is edible, and some peoples, notably the Fang of Central Africa, use elephant hide for their shields.

Some countries have reserves for Western game hunters. Permits are available for big game, small game and waterfowl. Regulations are strict. Hunters have to buy their bullets on the spot. There are open and close seasons, and even in the open season there are limits on the number of animals that can be shot.

In Senegal, a small game permit allows a hunter to shoot one warthog per week and 25 animals from any other species per day. A big game permit allows an extra warthog a week. There is also a 'bagging tax' to be paid on every animal shot. The tax for a buffalo is more than 500 euros. Special presidential authorisation is needed for hunting lion. The shooting of a female animal is penalised: the hunter has to pay double taxes. The same penalty applies if an animal is wounded, but not killed and manages to escape.

Triumphal returns *The small duiker antelope (above) is a popular prey for African hunters. Right: Hunters in Benoué National Park in Cameroon carry home a lion, carefully tied to a makeshift litter made from branches.*

Keeping things going: women in Africa

Women are the workers of Africa. It is hard to imagine how the continent could survive the vicissitudes of climate, political instability and fluctuating commodity prices without the labour of its women, who keep their families afloat through constant toil, in the home, fields and markets.

Piggyback *A woman in Cameroon carrying her baby on her back.*

It is rare to see a woman sitting down and taking it easy in Africa. For women, especially the women of the savannah, the day brings no respite in a constant stream of activity: children to look after, fields to work in, millet to pound . . . and a thousand other tasks.

In a continent where the men are frequently on the move, it is left to the women to keep the family together and ensure their day-to-day survival. The men may come home from a hunting trip empty-handed, or go off to the city in the hunt for jobs. The women, meanwhile, have to make sure there is enough to eat each day, usually with the help of the children, who are put to work at a tender age. When times are particularly bad, they may have to revert to the old gatherer way of life, collecting berries, seeds, even insects – grasshoppers in the savannah, termites in the forest zones. The nuts of the shea tree are always worth collecting: they produce a fat, known as shea butter, that can be sold as well as eaten.

Pounding and preparing millet porridge

Millet is the vital crop of the dry savannah, the only cereal that will grow with less than 18 in (450 mm) of rainfall a year. And, inevitably, it is the women who make the daily bowl of millet porridge – a dish so flavourless that only a spicy sauce makes it palatable. The men do the initial work, clearing the ground and ploughing it. Then the women take over, sowing, weeding, reaping and finally pounding the millet to get it into a form where they can begin to cook it – the pounding alone takes a good hour each day.

Hairdos *Women in Guinea dressing one another's hair.*

Age-old task *One of the immemorial sights of African village life is a woman pounding the millet – in this case on the Bissagos islands off Guinea-Bissau.*

Queens of the retail trade

Most of Central and West Africa's retail trade is carried out in markets and streetside stalls. And to a large extent it is this trade, dominated by women, that keeps the continent fed and clothed. In Togo's capital, Lomé, the market women sit on large iron trunks that contain their capital outlay and their hopes of profit, in the form of batik-style dyed cloths, known as *pagne*, that women wrap round their waists as skirts and men wear on formal occasions like a Roman toga. Their buyers may themselves be traders, who will take the textiles up to the savannah highlands, selling them on, with healthy mark-ups.

African markets: a drama of crowds, colour and aroma

Different regions have their specialities: seafood along the coasts; fruit in the forests; local crafts in other places, ranging from the carved wooden stools of the Ashanti to the butterfly masks of Burkina. What never changes in Africa's markets is their milling throngs of people.

Tasty crawlers *Traders in Kinshasa's central market sell huge forest caterpillars, which can be cooked with spices for a succulent meal.*

Makola market, in Accra, Ghana, specialises in colourful beads and fabrics. The nearby Obruni Wa Wu market, whose name means 'The white man has died', sells all manner of secondhand clothing. The market at Agadez, in Niger, is the best place for buying Tuareg leatherwork.

Bargains for early shoppers

Specialisation has been perpetuated in the markets of Africa by a transport system characterised by poor roads, sparse railways and a general scarcity of vehicles. And with little refrigeration in these tropical climes, the meat of animals slaughtered in the morning has to be sold within a few hours. The best thing is to get to the market early. Not only is the food freshest, but the first customers can be sure of the best prices. They are believed to bring luck – the earlier the customer, the better the luck for that day. The first customer served, the usual routine of fierce haggling begins. Between purchases, shoppers may mull over the day's news with friends. Then they may head for the corner of the market where the fetish-sellers spread their wares – for a love philtre, perhaps, or a potion against kidney stones or smallpox.

The market may cover a patch of open ground or take place in a huge hangar-like structure. In the Congo region, market traders include dressmakers, tailors, basketmakers, cabinetmakers and wonderfully versatile scrap-metal workers, capable of taking an old tin can and turning it into a funnel or a grater.

The snack-seller *A market woman in Bouaké, Ivory Coast, prepares maize fritters.*

Mosaic of colour *Mangoes, oranges, bananas, peppers, chilli pods and chilli powder, clothes – all these and more are bought and sold in Abidjan's Trechville market.*

Incense, spices and fish

Senegal's capital, Dakar, is famous for its markets. Even by African standards, these are thronging with people, brimful of colour and bustle. The smells, too, are intoxicating, ranging from the bewitching fragrance of the popular Senegalese incense, *thiouraye*, through the heady scents of spices and ripe mangoes, to the delicate aroma of fresh fish. The Kolobane market is reckoned to be the capital's most comprehensive, where stalls selling colour televisions, shoes, secondhand books, sacks of rice and cooked chickens, all jostle one another in a glorious jumble. Soumbédioune market sells the works of local artists and craftspeople, aimed at tourists. On the seashore, Yoff Plage has the capital's chief fish market. Fishermen in their dugout canoes sell their catches to the local women, who immediately sell them on, in glistening piles of tuna, sea trout, sea bream, grouper and mullet.

CHAPTER 3

RARE SIGHTS AND SECRET PLACES

The qualities of traditional African architecture are widely underrated. Using poor and often perishable materials – earth, mud bricks, straw and reeds – the builders create richly symbolic structures blending seamlessly with the landscape. In Africa, the individual home is commonly seen as feminine: fertile, protective, maternal. The layout of a village, too, can be symbolic. The principal villages of the Bamileke people of Cameroon follow an unchanging pattern that draws attention to the importance of the chief. The market square must stand in the correct place in relation to his palace and to the huts of his wives. Nowhere do the homes fit more perfectly into their surroundings than in the water communities of Lake Nokoué in southern Benin. Villages and towns of bamboo are built not beside the lake, but on it, raised on piles.

Posts sticking out from the mud walls of the minaret of the mosque at Agadez, Niger, are used during repair work.

Self-supporting *The huts of the Mousgoum people of Cameroon have no inner framework.*

Architecture: linking mankind with nature

Architecture in Africa is of a piece with nature. The building materials are dried mud and wooden branches. And the shapes and colours are just as organic. The curves of buildings recreate the outlines of the landscape. In a universe charged with meaning, the home and the way it is decorated help to establish harmony between people and the invisible forces of nature.

There are no straight lines or sharp angles in most traditional African homes. The walls are shaped by hand, and follow natural curves. Even doorways are oval, their edges smoothed over with clay, and symbolising the entrance to the womb. The way the home is decorated is linked to fertility. Inside the hut is the domain of the women; outside is the domain of the men, and the bush, beyond the village confines, is the domain of the spirits.

The first villages

This style of architecture, moulded around the people who live in the buildings and use them, is entirely African in its origins. Scholars used to think that it had been introduced to sub-Saharan Africa along with Islam in the 9th century. But more recent researches have revealed a pedigree going back to the 2nd millennium BC, at least. That is the date of the region's oldest-known urban settlements, some of which may have been home to several thousand inhabitants. These towns and villages lay scattered along the escarpment known as Dhar Tîchît and its continuation Dhar Oualâta in south-eastern Mauritania.

According to archaeologists, the settlements consisted of a group of compounds of varying shapes and sizes, each compound surrounded by a palisade and separated from the next one by an alleyway or small square. Compounds had areas or structures dedicated to different activities: a granary for storing millet, a cooking area, a living area, clay benches covered with matting, a workshop for scraping skins or making tools in stone or wood. In other words, they were laid out like any modern village of the African savannah, from the Atlantic to the Red Sea coast.

The spread of the Sahara forced farming communities, including those of Dhar Tîchît, southwards. But they did not abandon their social structures,

Bristling mosques

Western interest in the banco architecture of the savannahs dates back to the early 20th century when the French employed local builders to restore the mosque at Djenné. It had been in ruins since the Fulani conqueror Shehu Ahmadu Lobbo wrecked it in 1830, because he disapproved of the form of Islam practised there. Bristling with wooden branches, the mosque became symbolic of a unique style of architecture, also represented by mosques at Bobo-Dioulasso and Agadez and the tomb of the Askia dynasty at Gao. The branches give workers foot and handholds when replastering the outside each year after the rainy season.

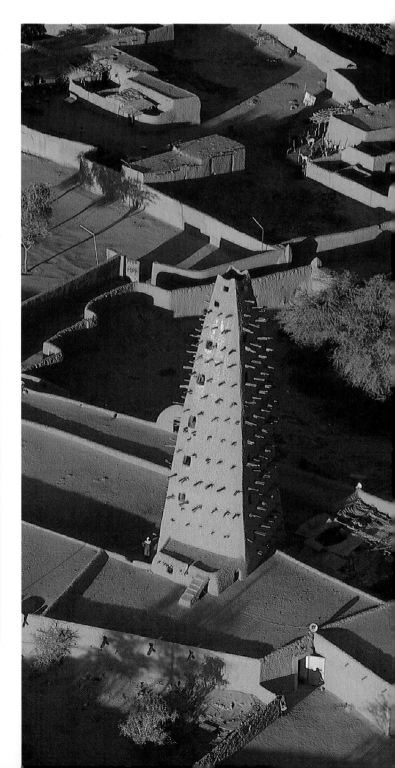

Mud minaret *The Songhai ruler Muhammad Askia built the mosque at Agadez in Niger around 1515.*

Cool courtyard   A family in the Casamance region of Senegal enjoy the shade. When rain falls, water is collected behind the low wall.

based on the extended family. Family groups still share a compound, where grandparents live alongside the different wives of the current head of the family, each wife with her own hut and her own fields to work.

Over the centuries, holy wars launched by Muslim peoples to convert their neighbours, as well as raids by marauding slave-hunters from the coast, created a climate of insecurity. Compounds huddled together to form large communities, sheltering behind walls of banco (sun-dried mudbrick). This form of defensive architecture is common to many of the animist peoples of West Africa, such as those around Bobo-Dioulasso in south-western Burkina. Where poor soil obliges communities to be more dispersed, each compound is a mini-fortress in its own right – as, for example, among the Tamberma and Kabyé peoples of northern Togo, the Somba of Benin and the Gurunsi of Burkina.

A city beneath the city

Aoudaghost in southern Mauritania was once a thriving trading city on the caravan routes crossing the Sahara. It was thought to have been built by Berber merchants from North Africa, but archaeological digs have unearthed, beneath the Berber city, the remains of stone and mudbrick compounds similar to those at Dhar Tîchît. Comparing the remains with modern villages, it seems possible that buildings of more than one storey may have existed in ancient Africa. Similar ancient remains have been found beneath the more recent structures of other great medieval cities, including Djenné, Ségou and Mopti on the Niger and Niani in Guinea, capital in the 13th and 14th centuries of the great empire of Mali.

In the forest zones, houses tend to be rectangular and built of banco. In the Casamance region of southern Senegal, with a high rainfall, they have thick thatch roofs to protect them. Some are specially designed to collect the rainwater. The roofs slope inwards, so that the rain flows down the slope and is collected into a pool in the central courtyard.

Sheltering roof   This conical straw 'hat' will be used to roof a granary in a Dogon village in Mali.

Millet stores

The granaries used to store millet are a fine example of the African gift for combining the decorative with the practical. For agrarian peoples, surviving in a harsh environment, reliable storage is vital. The granaries have to protect the harvest from both visible dangers – insects and rodents – and invisible ones: the forces of nature and the spirits which can unleash, for example, torrential rains. They are raised from the ground to keep the grain dry, and often shaped like giant human figures. Animals modelled in clay – for example, a snake, symbol of immortality – are believed to bring the protection of the spirits.

Hausa-style   Geometric patterns on a mosque in Kano, Nigeria, reflect the decorative traditions of the Hausa.

Dizzy survival in Dogon country

Defying the laws of gravity and the onslaughts of history, the villages of the Dogon people cling vertiginously to the Cliffs of Bandiagara in the Mopti region of Mali. The Dogon fled there in the 14th century AD when a new religion, Islam, was sweeping through the plains below. Many are still animists, and still living in houses built into the sheer cliff sides.

Child brides *More than one-third of the Dogon are now Muslim. As a result, child marriage is on the wane.*

Stairways dug out of the rock face snake their way up the Cliffs of Bandiagara. In some places, a ladder bridges a chasm, carved from the fork of a baobab tree that once grew in the plain below. Underneath opens the great dizzying emptiness. The Dogon have two remarkable achievements to their credit: they have tamed the void and learned how to eke out a living in an arid land.

The geometry of village building

For them, the cliffs have meant protection – from marauding Mossi, Songhai and Fulani raiders. Over the centuries, in their cliff refuges, they developed a style of building which they kept when they began to return to the plains. Huts are rectangular, cooking areas round and grain stores have conical straw caps. Family compounds and villages as a whole are arranged so that they represent the human body.

At the heart of a village is the Togu Na, or House of Words, where only the men are allowed. It consists of a roof perched on eight carved posts, eight being the number of mythical ancestors of the Dogon, as well as the number of wise men or elders in each village. The village's spiritual leader is the *hogon*, the priest of the serpent god Lebe, who according to myth led the Dogon from the Nile valley to their new cliff homes. The *hogon*'s hut is decorated with twisted columns, monkeys' skulls and precious stones. The image of Lebe also adorns the huts on the edge of the village where women go during menstruation.

In some villages, tourists are allowed to watch a few of the traditional masked dances of the Dogon. But they will be shooed away from the altars where people leave offerings for their ancestors. And the cave tombs gouged into the cliff faces above the villages are completely out of bounds. The bodies of the dead are hoisted up there on ropes; the special masks for the ritual dances are also stored here. In the 1930s the French ethnologist Marcel Griaule was initiated into the mysteries of Dogon beliefs, and after his death in 1956 he was accorded the rare honour for an outsider of being buried in one of the cave tombs.

Dogon country

Map showing: MAURITANIA, MALI, Timbuktu, Gao, Mopti, NIGER, Niamey, Bamako, Niger, Senegal, Bandiagara, BURKINA, GUINEA

Cliff homes *The Bandiagara escarpment stretches for more than 120 miles (200 km) and rises 660 to 980 ft (200 to 300 m) above the plain. Different African peoples have used it as a place of refuge since at least 300 BC. Of the 250 000 Dogon, some are plain-dwellers, but most still live in cliff villages.*

The water people of Lake Nokoué

For the Tofinu people of southern Benin, home is a lake. Their villages are built on piles above Lake Nokoué. They follow the rhythms of the fishing year in a world where, according to their traditional beliefs, the elements are controlled by voduns, *or spirits.*

Pushing through   *Vegetation clogs parts of the lake, but a boat is still the best, and often only, way of getting around.*

It is early dawn, and in the east, the sky is only just beginning to grow pale. But already the first dugout canoe is sliding across the still waters of the lake. A month ago it was *tohuba*, the point in the year during the dry season when the water level in the lake is at its lowest. It is now coming up to *obue* – mid January in the Western calendar – when the Tofinu men gather in the harvest of their *akajas*, fish farms devised by the people of Lake Nokoué.

Fish farming

The *akajas* are pens, created by driving tree branches into the muddy floor of the lake to fence off a portion of water. Here, fish and crayfish are trapped and fattened up for six months. When the time comes to gather in the harvest of freshwater sole, carp and other fish, the men drive sticks into the mud around the perimeter of the *akaja* and string a net, known as an *akajado*, between them. They then move the sticks and net inwards, tightening the noose around the trapped fish, until they are able to haul them into their canoes.

Today, the favour of Anasi Gbegu, the water *vodun*, must be with the fishermen, for they bring in a decent catch. But it is harder than it used to be. Only a narrow strip of land separates the lake from the waters of the Atlantic, and ever since the deep-water harbour at nearby Cotonou was completed in 1965, sea water has been seeping into the lake, increasing salinity and affecting fish stocks.

Some 50 000 Tofinu live in the lake's villages and towns, their homes of bamboo and corrugated iron, with reed-thatched roofs, raised above the water. Their ancestors chose this way of life – building 'on the waters where feet can no longer come' – to escape the slave-hunters of the kings of Abomey. The name of their capital, Ganvié, comes from the Tofinu word for 'saved'. Nowadays, however, they are under threat from the waters that once protected them. The lake has become contaminated as well as increasingly saline.

And yet, the life of the lake carries on. The fishermen come in with laden canoes, and soon they are surrounded by women, who haggle over the catch, then shoot off across the waters to Ganvié, where their dugouts become floating stalls in a floating market.

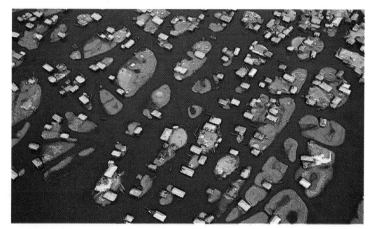

African Venice   *Only 9 miles (15 km) from Cotonou, Ganvié is Africa's largest lake town.*

The spirits of the lake

Traditionally, the Tofinu have been keen followers of the *vodun* cult of Benin. To communicate with the *voduns*, ceremonies known as *kokou* are organised, when the spirits come down and, amid drumming and dancing, take possession of souls. Nowadays, however, the ceremonies are becoming rarer, because of the opposition of an evangelical Christian sect, the Celestial Church of Christ, which has had considerable success among the Tofinu.

Shopping on the water
The market at Ganvié is accessible only by canoe.

Gorée island: a sinister beauty

Just off the Senegalese coast, facing the capital, Dakar, is an enchanted isle haunted by horrific memories. The tiny island of Gorée, just over a mile (1.6 km) long, caressed by the trade winds and bathed by crystal-clear waters, was the place from which thousands of Africans were shipped across the Atlantic as slaves.

Journey without return *Slaves, plundered on the nearby continent, passed along corridors like this on their way to the continent across the Atlantic.*

The blaze of bougainvilleas trailing from walls, old houses elegantly colourwashed in a range of ochre hues – it all adds to a bewitching beauty, much appreciated by the *jeunesse dorée* of Dakar, who like to come out to Gorée to play.

A pawn in the slave trade

Yet this tranquil charm cannot blot out the island's shameful past, when it was a pawn in the commercial rivalry among the European powers. From the 16th century, it belonged in turn to the Portuguese, the Dutch, the French and, for a short while, the British – all drawn by a safe anchorage (the name Gorée probably derives from the Dutch *goede reede*, 'good roads',

meaning 'sea roads'), close to the African coast but facing out across the Atlantic to the Americas. The French seized the island in 1677, and under them it became a major base for trans-shipping slaves bound for France's West Indian colonies.

Nowadays, one of the island's principal tourist sites is the House of Slaves with its 'gate from which no one returned'. Some historians have downplayed the island's importance in the slave trade.

Certainly, any slaves shipped from here would have represented only a tiny fraction of the total number traded along Africa's western coast from Senegal in the north to Angola in the south. Yet, whatever the accounting, Gorée has become symbolic of a traffic in human souls whose consequences still weigh heavily on the present.

A place by the sea *Houses with tiled roofs, shady verandahs and large gardens help to make modern Gorée a fashionable resort.*

Bitter memories

Many of the modern visitors to Gorée's House of Slaves are African-Americans. It is a well set-up tourist site with signs indicating the cells where the slaves were kept and the room where they were weighed. And yet the overwhelming impression it leaves behind is of suffering: the humiliation inflicted on human beings snatched from their native lands. The island's fortunes declined from the mid 19th century. But a century and a half later, it is still impregnated with the memory of a tragic trade that bound together the fates of four continents – Africa, the Americas and Europe.

Island charm *Gorée's 18th-century houses have a well-preserved elegance.*

Bandjoun: a jewel in the highlands

The Bamileke of Cameroon are famous for their wood carving, their masks made of beads and their chefferies –
villages of the chiefs. Bandjoun is the largest of these and the one where the ancient arts have survived best.

A Bamileke chief is called a *fon*, and for half a century until 1975 the Fon of Bandjoun was Joseph Kamga II, an enthusiastic moderniser, who built two hospitals within his realms, three secondary schools and several primary schools. He himself provided many of the pupils: over the course of a long lifetime he fathered no fewer than 250 children.

Where the old ways live on

Bandjoun today keeps rigorously to the traditional ways of a Bamileke chiefdom. Scattered over its territory are a number of small communities known as *tandios*. At its centre is Bandjoun itself, housing the palace of the *fon* and other important communal buildings. Visitors enter the settlement through a double gateway, which is flanked on either side by huts with pointed roofs. Beyond that lies the market square, around which the rest of the village spreads out.

As with the 'capitals' of all Bamileke chiefdoms, Bandjoun is built on a slope, the *kouoh-tsa*. The huts of the *fon*'s wives are at the lower end of the slope. At the top is the central hut, the scene of the chiefdom's important ceremonial occasions. In Bandjoun this stands 65 ft (20 m) high and was built in the 18th century by Fon Nghoto.

At the front, where the roof juts out, is a high verandah, supported by wooden posts carved with scenes from the everyday life of the chiefdom and from its history. The bamboo walls have elaborate geometric patterns engraved on them. A collection of items inside is evidence of a sophisticated artistic tradition and includes gourds and statues encrusted with pearls and other jewels, ivory figurines, masks and sumptuous feather headdresses.

Ceremonial centre Bandjoun's central hut, one of the wonders of Bamileke country.

Forest style, savannah style

The Bamileke use the traditions of the rain forest to build the walls of their homes. The basic framework consists of bamboo poles with plant fibres woven between them; over this is laid a plaster of dried mud known as *poto-poto*. The door has a carved wooden frame and is raised 20 in (50 cm) off the ground to prevent water draining into the hut, as well as to keep out unwelcome insects and snakes. The roof is conical and made from thatch – in the tradition of the savannah.

Mask finery Dancers during a Bamileke festival wear colourful masks adorned with glass beads.

CHAPTER 4

POVERTY IN THE MIDST OF PLENTY

The vast region of Central and West Africa is richly endowed with natural resources, but millions of its inhabitants live in poverty. Drought, ethnic tensions and the legacy of colonialism have all helped to keep Africa in the developing world. Yet there is much that gives hope for tomorrow. Africa has a wealth of valuable mineral resources, including oil, gold, zinc, phosphates, uranium and copper. Sometimes, however, the very abundance of riches can lead to problems. Nigeria, for example, which depends on oil for 90 per cent of its export earnings, has experienced an ecological disaster in the oil-producing Niger delta. The produce of farms and plantations is as important as that of mines and oil wells. Cotton, cocoa and coffee are major exports, while many of the fruits and vegetables enjoyed in the homes and restaurants of Europe, from bananas to mangoes, papayas and passion fruit, were grown in Africa.

Lovingly tended vegetable plots in the Sahel keep the advancing Sahara at bay.

Farming – from subsistence to growing for the market

The traditional African family or village is self-sufficient, growing enough food to meet its needs. This pattern was disrupted in many places during colonial times, when land was turned over to crops such as coffee and cocoa, for which there was a demand in the West. Farmers in Africa still grow for that market, but in recent times a new kind of agriculture has emerged: market gardening for expanding towns and cities.

Old-style transport *Agriculture in West Africa is still largely unmechanised.*

Sun, good soil and rain are basic requirements if crops are to flourish, and Central and West Africa have an abundant supply of only one of these – sunshine. The supply of cultivable land faces a double threat, from population growth and from the advance of the Saharan sands. Rainfall is uneven: it drenches the tropical forests, but droughts are commonplace elsewhere.

Agriculture remains an important economic activity – in Burkina by far the most important. Around 90 per cent of the population work on the land, producing large quantities of two key cereal crops: sorghum and millet. But very little of this is exported: almost the entire harvest is consumed locally. Gabon, by contrast, focuses on crops grown for export, such as cocoa, coffee and sugar. The revenues from its oil fields mean that it can afford to import food that is not grown locally. Within the next few decades, however, its oil reserves are likely to run low, and the government is trying to bring Burkina back to being more self-sufficient in food production.

Tomato-flavoured porridge

Rice, beans, sorghum, yams and tomatoes are all grown in Niger, but the biggest crop is millet. The seeds are used to make flour or semolina, the stems fed to livestock as hay. One of the most popular dishes in Niger is *tuwo* – millet flour boiled to make a porridge, then seasoned with a tomato or okra-based sauce.

In Mali, the region in the far west of the country, watered by the upper reaches of the Sénégal river, grows aubergines, beetroots, carrots, cucumbers, peppers, lettuces, okra, tomatoes, lemons and oranges. Farther east, the Dogon plateau is renowned for its vegetables, and central Mali has one of the oldest and largest irrigation systems in sub-Saharan Africa, the so-called Office du Niger scheme, set up by the French in the 1930s. The zone it covers produces 53 000 tons of shallots a year. Around 6000 tons of onions are grown in the Bamako basin in the south-west of the country

Life-giving river   Vegetable plots line the Sénégal river near Kayes in western Mali. Crops and human populations alike are concentrated along the banks of rivers.

Fields of fame *Onions grown by the Dogon people of Mali are specially prized for their flavour.*

and in market gardens around the towns and cities. Rice contributes 4-5 per cent of the GDP and is a key element in the government's plan for the country to produce enough food to feed itself.

All across the Sahel, the enemies of agriculture are the southward expansion of the Sahara and a bone-dry climate – in some places, the dry season lasts for eight months a year. Another problem is the rising population. Desperate to produce more food to feed the extra mouths, villagers cut corners. Land is not allowed to lie fallow long enough for it to recover from intensive cropping, key nutrients are not restored to the soil and grazing animals make the vegetation cover even thinner.

This sets up a process of erosion which can end in desertification. In Burkina, the government has established information centres and regional nurseries in its efforts to encourage better farming practices in the country.

Staple *Millet is a staple food in West Africa. Pearl millet, in particular, is well suited to dry climates and soils with low fertility.*

Fighting erosion

In zones where the soil has become most depleted, they have planted belts of vegetation to try to halt erosion and they encourage the creation of family or village vegetable plots. By this means, they seek to establish a common food store in each community, to make sure that even the poorest will always have enough to eat. They also send advisers to supervise the work in the village plots.

Keeping the country green
In Burkina, tiny plots like this, fenced off to keep out wild animals, are a key weapon in the struggle against desertification.

Flavoursome onions from Dogon country

The Bandiagara cliffs rise high above the plains of central Mali. Cliffs paths make their way through gaps, across piles of fallen rock and along narrow gorges as they link the plains below with the plateau above. And in amongst them, tiny vegetable plots are planted in countless nooks and crannies. Pockets of cultivable soil are terraced, and mini-dams built to create ponds for irrigation. Here, the local people, the Dogon, grow carrots, potatoes and, above all, famously tasty onions. On market days, heavily laden Dogon women head along the paths to the town of Sangha to sell their produce.

The bitter-sweet allure of chocolate

Dark, rich and comforting, chocolate has been one of the small luxuries of life in every nation since the Spanish introduced it into Europe from the Americas in the 16th century. Chocolate and cocoa come from the fruit of the cacao tree, which grows only in the tropics.

Picking the pods *A harvester gathering the crop in Cameroon.*

A good 40 per cent of the world's cocoa comes from Ivory Coast. Its production – 1.2 million tons in 2001 – far outstrips any other country's, but this also brings a dangerous dependency: its economy is very sensitive to the ups and downs of world cocoa prices, which are largely in the control of the multinational chocolate companies. When, in 2001, the cocoa farmers of Ivory Coast were accused of using child slaves, members of the government pointed the finger of blame at the chocolate companies. It was they, the ministers said, who kept prices low, driving farmers into poverty: in some cases, farmers resorted to forced labour.

Cameroon grows a relatively modest 5 per cent of world production. The overall harvest is still large: 115,000 tons in 2001, the bulk from small family-run plantations. Some 60 per cent of plantations cover less than 2.5 acres (1 ha). Farmers tend to grow cocoa alongside ordinary food crops, and so avoid over-dependence on a single crop. For the most part, they farm organically, not so much from choice, but because they cannot afford to buy expensive machinery or artificial fertilisers.

Generally speaking, cocoa is grown on a small scale in the countries of West Africa, with growers

For export *Sackloads of cocoa being loaded onto a ship in Ivory Coast's chief port, Abidjan.*

organised into cooperatives. Buyers from the big chocolate companies go from plantation to plantation purchasing directly from the farmers or their cooperatives.

From the tree to the table

The cacao tree (*Theobroma cacao*) is native to the Americas, where it was first cultivated and chocolate first consumed. It now grows in humid lowland areas throughout the tropics. Humidity is essential: it needs a humidity level of 90 per cent to thrive.

It is fast-growing: a three-year-old cacao tree stands 10-16 ft (3-5 m) high and a mature tree is around 26 ft (8 m) high. The pod (fruit) is 4-10 in (10-25 cm) long and $2^{1}/_{2}$-$4^{3}/_{4}$ in (6-12 cm) in diameter; it can weigh from 10 oz (300 g) to 18 oz (500 g). A tree may bear between 25 and 100 pods in a year, and each pod contains 25 to 75 cocoa beans, nestling in a pink pulp.

When harvested, the pods are split open and the beans placed in crates, where they are left to ferment for a few days. This allows the full chocolate flavour to develop. The beans are then spread out to dry, usually in the sun. They are cleaned to get rid of the remains of pulp, then they are sorted, roasted and ground. The result is a thick paste known as chocolate liquor. This is then pressed to make either cocoa powder or cocoa butter, the basic ingredient of the chocolate that goes on sale in sweetshops all over the world.

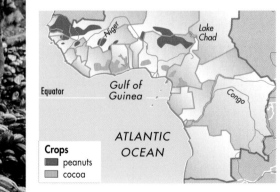

Shelling beans *A worker splits open cocoa pods on the island of Bioko, Equatorial Guinea.*

Tasty snack A boy selling
peanut sticks in Benin.

Harvests of nuts

Peanuts are best known in the West as salty snacks for nibbling at parties, in bars or on plane journeys. But, like Africa's cashews and coconuts, they have many other uses – from producing cooking oil to providing a protein-rich feed for livestock.

Africa accounts for around 20 per cent of the world's production of peanuts. And the farmers of West Africa, particularly of Senegal, claim that their peanuts have a better flavour than those of any other region on Earth. Peanuts are not just for export; they are a key element in African cookery. They are roasted in the sun or in sand and then sold on the streets; they are also used in a popular sauce that accompanies many local dishes.

Ripening under the ground

Peanuts come from the vine *Arachis hypogaea*, also known as the groundnut vine because of the way it grows. The stalks bend over and grow back into the soil, which is where the seedpods ripen. In common with other local crops, the produce of the groundnut vine has varied uses. The cotton plant produces cotton, of course, but also an oil, extracted from the cotton seeds, and the dried meat of the coconut, known as copra, produces coconut oil. Groundnuts can be eaten as peanuts or pressed to extract oil, used in cooking and to make soap. The residue, after pressing, is made into 'cake' for livestock.

The palm family includes around 2800 species worldwide. Common species in West Africa include the African oil palm (*Elaeis guineensis*), whose seeds are pressed to extract palm kernel oil, used in cooking, in margarine and vegetable butter, in the manufacture of soaps and cosmetics and as a lubricant in machinery. As with

Pounding for oil Men in Guinea-Bissau pound the seed of the oil palm to extract the oil.

groundnuts, the residue can be used to make cattle cake. The giant, overtopping all other West African palms, is the fan palm (*Borassus aethiopum*), which can grow to be 82 ft (25 m) high. Its wood is to a large extent rot-proof and termite-proof, and is often used to make the frames for buildings. Its leaves are used to make brooms and as thatch for roofs. The sap of both palmyra and oil palms is used to make palm wine.

Palm wine

The so-called terminal bud, at the very top of the palmyra palm, can be tapped to obtain a sweet sap. This is either drunk fresh or allowed to ferment to create an alcoholic drink which is popular during village festivities.

The person who obtains the sap is a respected figure in the community. Using a hoop to attach himself to the trunk, he clambers nimbly to the top of the palm, almost as if he were walking up it. At the top, he sticks a straw tube into the terminal bud and catches the sap in a suitable receptacle. The other villagers pay him in money or rice.

Prize produce Senegalese peanuts are processed and packed into sacks, ready for export.

Fruit and vegetables, in season and out

Many of the exotic fruits sold in European supermarkets and greengrocers' shops come from Africa – papayas, mangoes, starfruit, passion fruit among them. Another development in recent decades has been growing out-of-season vegetables, again for export. In winter, for example, the best fresh green beans are likely to have been grown in Mali.

Red hot *Fiery hot to the European palate, chilli peppers are a common ingredient in African cooking. These come from Niger.*

Market gardening began in Africa, as in Europe, around the larger towns and cities. Busy townspeople were willing to pay good prices for food they could not grow themselves. As transport improved, African produce could be shipped farther, especially to Europe, where there was an expanding market for exotic or out-of-season fruit and vegetables. Particular areas became known for particular crops – Kongoussi in Burkina for its tomatoes,

for example, and Mali for its green beans. In many places, export markets have become as important as local ones.

Mali exported 820 tons of mangoes in 2000. Its biggest markets were France, Britain, Germany, Belgium, the Netherlands – and the United Arab Emirates. In green beans, it exported a more modest 150 tonnes – compared with nearly 11 000 tons from Niger and 2600 tons from Burkina. But quality made up for quantity. In the produce markets of Europe, Mali's green beans are reckoned to have the finest flavour of any.

On the other hand, as in other African countries, the export trade in Mali's fruit and vegetables is largely controlled by multinational companies, who are frequently accused of creaming off the bulk of the profits, paying low prices to the farmers and causing environmental damage because of the unsustainable farming practices they encourage.

Exotic fruits

Despite the familiarity of European consumers with the produce of the tropics, a visit to an African market will still spring many surprises. These may include an array of the knobbly green fruits known as soursops, with their refreshing, slightly acid-tasting flesh, and calabashes. When the calabash's flesh is scooped out, the shell can be used as a salad bowl or ladle – or as the resonance chamber of a stringed instrument.

But the continent's biggest fruit exports by far are bananas and pineapples. The two most commonly grown species of banana are the dessert banana (*Musa sapientum*) and the plantain (*Musa paradisiaca*), which is usually eaten cooked to accompany fish or meat dishes. Plantains can be boiled, fried, grilled or made into a porridge. Or they

Secret of the burning bush

Unlike many of Africa's food and drink exports, coffee is a native species. The arabica variety originated in Ethiopia, while the robusta comes from the Congo basin. The continent's three biggest exporters are Ivory Coast, Uganda and Ethiopia, with other significant exports from Togo, Cameroon, Congo-Kinshasa and the Central African Republic.

According to an African tale, coffee-drinking began after a fire set light to some bushes, whose berries, as they burned, gave off a delicious aroma. Once the fire was over, local farmers gathered up the burnt berries, ground them and made them into a drink – which has remained popular ever since.

One way of processing the coffee is to place the picked berries in racks in layers about 2 in (5 cm) thick. The racks are shaken several times a day to let the air circulate. If a worker picks up a handful of berries and can hear the beans rattling inside them, he knows that they are ready for the next stage, during which they are sorted and the beans separated from the pulp of the berry – using a pestle or mechanically. Another process involves immersing the berries in tanks of water. The good berries

float, and then have the pulp removed. The beans are left to ferment for 12 to 36 hours, depending on the surrounding temperature.

It takes huge acreages of bushes to satisfy the world's thirst for coffee. In most years, a coffee bush will produce about 5.5 lb (2.5 kg) of berries, and these will yield just 14 oz (400 g) of coffee. So a little over 6½ lb (3 kg) of berries have to be picked for every 18 oz (500 g) packet of coffee.

Red berries *Angolan coffee.*

can be dried and made into a flour, which is then used to make bread or baby food.

The pineapple originated in the Americas and was not introduced into Africa until the late 19th century. But it soon made itself at home. Ivory Coast is now one of the world's biggest exporters in the world. The fruit, with its topknot of small leaves, grows on the ground at the centre of a rosette of spiky leaves, which can be up to 3 ft 3 in (1 m) long. It has to be harvested young to make sure that it is fresh when it reaches the overseas markets. It is also very delicate: a bruise when harvesting or during transport is likely to spoil the entire pineapple. The harvesting is all done by hand, with the fruit packed into specially padded crates.

Easy does it Pineapple harvesting in Ivory Coast – delicate work, for bruising could be disastrous.

African spinach N'dolé, or bitter leaf (above), is a spinach-like vegetable grown in Cameroon. It is cooked with peanuts, garlic and spices.

Balancing act Women in Congo-Kinshasa's Ituri region (above) carry produce to the weekly market, balancing it on their heads.

Rice paddies The Casamance region in southern Senegal has a hot and humid climate, suitable for growing rice.

King Cotton in West Africa

West Africa produces some of the world's finest quality cotton, much of it exported direct to Asia, where it is woven into cloth. Mali is the leading local exporter of this 'white gold', but other important producers include Burkina, Benin, Ivory Coast, Cameroon and Chad.

The cotton pickers *Enamel basins, baskets and sacks serve to bring in the harvest on the small plantations where most of West Africa's cotton is grown.*

Cotton, introduced by Western explorers and missionaries in the 19th century, is vital for the future of Mali. The country relies heavily on its earnings from cotton exports to finance improvements in other sectors of the economy.

It was only in the 1960s that cotton became a truly profitable crop, but Mali is now the largest producer in sub-Saharan Africa and, after Egypt, the second-largest in the entire continent. Most of its harvest of more than 500 000 tons a year comes from small-scale plantations of less than 2.5 acres (1 ha).

Burkina, the region's second-largest producer, has a harvest of around 180 000 tons a year, of which a proportion is spun and woven into cloth in mills set up by the French in the Bobo region in the south-west of the country. In Cameroon, it is estimated that as many as a million people – out of a total population of 15.7 million – depend for their living, either directly or indirectly, on the cotton industry.

The French presence

One legacy of the years of French rule in West Africa is that in most countries the processing of locally grown cotton is controlled by a state monopoly, acting through a single company. But a strong current of opinion is now running in favour of privatisation and the introduction of competition. This thinking is opposed by the *Compagnie française pour le developpement des fibres textiles* (CFDFT), set up in 1949, with the French state as its majority shareholder, to promote the cotton industry in France's West African colonies.

After the various territories gained their independence, the CFDFT remained an inescapable presence. It gave technical advice and was often a substantial shareholder in the successor companies set up in each state. To this day, the CFDFT trains the small-scale cotton farmers, provides credit, seed, fertilisers and insecticides and supervises the harvesting and processing of the crop.

This monopolistic approach ensures that the different countries, rather than multinational companies, keep a large measure of control over their cotton industries, but it finds no favour with bodies such as the World Bank and the International Monetary Fund, which set a high value on competition.

Piled high *Bales are loaded onto a truck in the north of Ivory Coast.*

The many uses of cotton

After the cotton plant's cream-coloured flowers have bloomed, they leave small green seedpods or 'bolls'. Each boll contains between 20 and 50 seeds, and expands as the fibres grow inside, until eventually it bursts open. Once harvested, the fibres have to be separated from the seeds in a process known as 'ginning'. They are then cleaned, carded (brushed out and straightened) and spun into yarn. The finest quality fibres – the longest – are also combed, to straighten them still further. The seeds are pressed to extract cottonseed oil, used as a cooking fat and in the manufacture of soap. The residue is made into oil 'cake', used as feed for animals. It can also be made into a protein-rich flour.

Asia-bound *Once cleaned, carded and spun, the cotton is exported to Asia.*

The herders: a tradition under threat

For hundreds of years, peoples such as the Fulani and the Tuareg have lived as herders of cattle, camels and other livestock. Nowadays, however, their nomadic or seminomadic traditions are threatened. Many are obliged to adopt a settled way of life, which often leads to overgrazing by their herds and provokes the hostility of local farmers.

In the Central African Republic, a land with a population of just 3.8 million people, the total head of livestock has risen to more than 3 million cattle, 2.6 million goats, 680 000 pigs and 220 000 sheep. And the proportion of livestock to people is increasing, for the number of animals being slaughtered for meat is declining. A similar trend can be seen in Chad.

There are a number of reasons for this disparity, including a lack of properly equipped abattoirs and refrigerated warehouses. Another factor lies in the traditions of the region's herders, peoples such as the Fulani. For them, their herds are their wealth, treasured property to be passed on from generation to generation, rather than to be slaughtered for gain. Paradoxically, while livestock are underexploited, the land on which the growing herds graze is being overexploited. This is partly the result of state frontiers imposed in colonial times. Peoples who once wandered freely over huge swathes of West Africa now find their movements restricted.

Armful of status For the Fulani, livestock represent a family's wealth and standing.

Conflicting lifestyles

Tensions between the former nomads now obliged to adopt a more sedentary lifestyle and farmers in the zones where they settle are inevitable. Of the nearly 1235 million acres (500 million ha) of eroded or degraded land in Africa, more than a half is caused by overgrazing. One possible solution is to open corridors between the pasturing areas used by the herders in the dry and rainy seasons. These could cross national boundaries. In this way, the needs of both the herders and the environment could be accommodated. It would, however, require almost unprecedented levels of cooperation among representatives of the herders, the farmers, governments and international organisations.

When herds decline – or expand

Burkina suffered badly in the great droughts of 1974 and 1984, and among the worst hit were its Fulani inhabitants who saw their huge herds decimated. The herding tradition survives in Burkina, but is nothing like as important as it once was. In Cameroon, by contrast, the national head of livestock has risen in recent years, standing in 2001 at nearly 6 million cattle, 4.4 million goats and 1.4 million pigs. In neighbouring Gabon, the number of cattle has shrunk, partly through poor veterinary care and a shortage of drugs. Poultry farming, however, is on the increase, reflecting the eating habits of the Gabonese who, it seems, cannot get enough chicken. This may be because their chickens, almost always free range, are cheap and tasty.

Survivors Where they can, the Bororo Fulani people of Niger hold onto their nomadic lifestyle.

Living by the bounty of river, lake and sea

African fishermen still wrest a living from the sea, despite severe competition from the well-equipped trawler fleets of Spain, Japan, Russia and other nations, fishing on an industrial scale. Inland, some unique fishing communities have grown up along the banks of the continent's rivers and lakes.

Fisherman's pride *A fisherman from the Cape Verde islands carries his catch of tuna, the principal export fish.*

Foreign fleets, equipped with modern technology, rake through the rich fishing grounds of the Gulf of Guinea and its surrounding waters. But enough is left for the small-scale local fishermen to make Africa a significant exporter of shrimps, prawns, langoustines and, above all, tuna. Plenty, too, is kept for home consumption: the markets of coastal towns and cities display mouth-wateringly varied arrays of fish and shellfish.

Fishing bolsters the economy of many African countries. Every year, the sub-Saharan region exports hundreds of thousands of tons of dried fish. Getting it to market is in many places a creaky procedure, but efforts are being made to modernise processing and packaging plants – particularly important since the climate demands that catches should be frozen or dried in the shortest possible time.

Political and economic complications create their own problems. In the territorial waters of Congo (Brazzaville), for example, the zones set aside for fishing have been reduced in order to increase the zones for oil exploration, and the search for oil has taken precedence over the age-old rights of fishermen. The fishing industry of Equatorial Guinea suffered a sharp decline in its catch in 1998. In part, this was due to a shortage of vital tackle, from motors to nets to refrigeration equipment. Another factor was an outbreak of terrorist violence by a separatist movement on the island of Bioko, an important base for the country's fishing fleet.

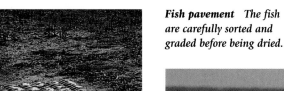

Fish pavement *The fish are carefully sorted and graded before being dried.*

Setting out *Before heading out into the open sea, fishermen have to master the surf as the waves break on the shore.*

The freshwater fishers

The lakes and rivers of the interior abound in the variety of their fish. Notable among these are the string of lakes down the length of the Great Rift Valley: Lake Tanganyika alone contains nearly 250 different species. Africans have always exploited this food source. In Congo (Brazzaville), almost every river, lake and backwater is a scene of activity as fishermen busy themselves with their lines, nets or traps.

A curious feature along the banks of many of the major rivers of the northern Congo basin is whole settlements raised above the water level on stilts. For much of the year they are deserted, but starting in May they fill up as fishermen and their families pour out of towns such as Mossaka, on the northern bank of the Congo, and head for the banks of the Songha, Likouala, Alima, Bokosso and Ndeko. Here they live for the next few months. They even clear patches of the riverside vegetation to create terraced vegetable plots. The fishing season comes to an end when the river level rises again; the fishers and their families pack up their belongings and return to the towns they came from. Throughout the season, they have been smoking their catch – their smoked fish is a great delicacy and will be sold in markets across the region and beyond.

Sure footed *Nimbleness is essential when setting fish traps in the Boyoma (formerly Stanley) Falls on the Congo.*

Africa's fisherwomen

In Cameroon, it is often the women who do the fishing. In many cases, they use nets. But they employ a variety of other techniques as well, many of them ancient. Sometimes they place traps with bait inside them in the middle of reed beds; this is a good way of catching eels, catfish and carp. Sometimes, more laboriously, they dam off whole sections of a pond or lake or even of a stream, using tree trunks, pebbles and clay to build the dams. They then empty the dammed-off section, standing in a line, singing and rhythmically scooping the water out, using wooden containers. The fish, trapped in a smaller and smaller pool of water, are easy to pull out. Even simpler is to throw narcotics into the water. The drugged fish float to the surface.

On the beach *Fishing boats pulled up at Soumbédioune in Senegal.*

A forest heritage endangered by need and greed

For the naturalist, or even the ordinary tourist, the tropical rain forests of sub-Saharan Africa are alive with surprises, wonders and discoveries. But their importance is more than scientific. The rain forests are a key economic resource – and one that is being seriously overexploited.

Slash and burn in Sierra Leone *Ground that has been cleared by fire is particularly vulnerable to erosion.*

The primary rain forests are getting smaller every day. Land-hungry farmers clear them to grow their crops; villagers fell trees for firewood. Above all, multinational logging companies move in, eager to exploit the precious hardwoods prized by furniture-makers and builders across the world. For tens of thousands of years, the people of the forests have made inroads on them, through slash-and-burn agriculture. But in the past, populations were smaller, and nature always had time to recover. Today, the ancestral forests of sub-Saharan Africa are under threat as never before.

Under pressure from environmentalists and international organisations, measures have been taken to curb the activities of the logging companies. At the same time, African governments also see the forests are ways of providing employment and increasing export revenues. In some countries, timber can be sold on the international market only if it has been processed in local sawmills. Although many of these are European or Asian-owned, at least the labour is local. Some governments are encouraging a local furniture-making industry, its products aimed at the export market.

Riches in wood

But the grip of the foreign companies remains formidable. In Congo (Brazzaville), for example, German, Swiss, French, Algerian and Libyan companies all control vast acreages of the rain forest, exporting a range of exotic woods, including mahogany, limba, sapele, sipo and pertmi. In Gabon, rain forest covers nearly two-thirds of the country – around 89 000 sq miles (230 000 km²) in all. The trees growing there include gaboon, one of the world's

Toppling a giant *Of the immense forests that once covered the south of Ivory Coast, only 5 million acres (2 million ha) remain.*

largest trees, growing up to 130 ft (40 m) tall, and the ironwood (or azobé) tree, whose wood is so dense that it sinks in water, like metal. The forests of Ivory Coast have more than 225 species, including mahogany, ebony, teak, iroko, obéché and samba. In recent years, the government has imposed tighter rules and regulations on the logging companies. But before that, in the 40 years from 1956 to 1996, five-sixths of the country's rain forest disappeared.

A balanced approach

The challenge facing Africa is how to safeguard the needs of both the economy and the environment. In 1990, the African Development Bank laid down a policy aimed at halting the deforestation of the continent. It stressed the importance of stabilising population growth and eradicating rural poverty, both of which put pressure on the forests. It also encouraged the setting up of local timber industries and forest wildlife reserves – similar to the reserves of the savannahs. Another concern was to protect the dry woodlands of the savannahs by planting fast-growing trees with the bank providing the finance.

In other parts of Africa, UNESCO's Man and the Biosphere programme creates reserves where the human population is seen as an integral part of the forest ecosystem. The World Bank, meanwhile, penalises states that encourage deforestation and the commercial exploitation of primary rain forest. To balance such deterrents, it finances schemes for managing the forests better, for planting trees and for extending forest reserves and national parks. In many cases, these measures have come too late, particularly in Ghana, Nigeria and Liberia, where the destruction of the rain forests has reached an advanced stage. Gabon, Congo (Brazzaville) and Congo (Dem. Rep.) are better placed: in these countries, much of the forest is still intact.

The Pygmies: guardians of the forest

The Pygmy peoples, who live in the great expanse of rain forest that spreads out over Congo-(Brazzaville), the Democratic Republic of Congo, Cameroon and the Central African Republic, have simple but effective ways of tapping the forest's riches. When they hunt they string nets between tree trunks; they then beat the forest wildlife towards the trees, where bush pigs, antelopes, and other animals become entangled in the nets. Their weapons include spears, bows and poison-tipped arrows. They also fish and gather honey, wild berries, mushrooms and edible roots. In the evenings, outside their huts made of leaves and branches, they sing and dance to appease the spirits of the forest. They are careful not to abuse the natural bounty that surrounds them: they never pick all the berries on a bush and never stay too long in any one hunting area.

At the sawmill Wood is loaded onto a truck at Bayanga in the Central African Republic. The mill exports valuable woods such as mahogany.

Making money In the forest regions, the logging industry has taken over from the banned ivory trade as a key source of revenue.

Greening the Sahel These seedlings in a nursery in Burkina will later be replanted in an endeavour to reforest the Sahel.

Ready for export Huge logs float in the harbour of San-Pédro (left), in western Ivory Coast, from where they will be exported.

Oil highway Pipelines near Port Harcourt, Nigeria.

Oil in Africa: riches for the few

Central and West Africa is rich in oil reserves, with Nigeria, Angola and Gabon as its leading producers. But an oil bonanza can devastate the environment, and the wealth it creates in these countries is often not evenly distributed.

Where the pickings are so great, corruption is perhaps inevitable. Major international oil companies have been accused of propping up some distinctly undemocratic regimes in Africa in return for lucrative contracts – for both the companies and the leaders of the regimes.

The peoples of the Niger delta, where the great river flows into the Gulf of Guinea, once lived by fishing in its multitude of criss-crossing waterways. Now the waterways are dead, the delta ecosystem ruined by pollution from the oil industry. In the 1960s, a good half of government oil revenues was channelled back into the delta and its communities. Nowadays, barely 10 per cent goes back. There are no fish left to catch, and poverty is increasing.

Fighting for survival

In 1992, the Ogoni people, led by journalist Ken Saro-Wiwa, founded the Movement for the Survival of the Ogoni People (MOSOP). In the words of Saro-Wiwa, 'The Ogoni people have now decided to make a last-ditch stand against the government and against Shell that have ripped them off for the last 35 years.' The government response was brutal. Saro-Wiwa was executed in November 1995, after a hastily arranged trial. In 1997, another Delta people, the Ijaw, launched their own protests. In part, these were a response to changes in the way local government was organised: oil revenues ploughed back into the region no longer went to communities as a whole, but to particular ethnic groups,

and the Ijaw felt discriminated against. There were violent confrontations between Ijaw protesters and government forces and a number of foreign oil workers were taken hostage.

Cruel paradoxes abound. Nigeria is one of the top 15 oil producers in the world – higher in the list than Kuwait and Libya – yet suffers from regular fuel shortages. Despite its oil riches, the most populous country in Africa is also one of the poorest. In the wake of Saro-Wiwa's execution, many international environmental and human rights bodies called for a boycott of Nigerian oil, claiming that the country's current political system was irredeemably corrupt.

Concerned by negative publicity, the oil companies sought to redeem their reputations. The city of Warri, centre of the Ijaw protests, is a dusty place, where run-down buildings huddle around a few churches and seedy bars. Three rival ethnic groups live in the region, the Ijaw, the Urhobo and the Itsekiri – alongside foreign oil workers, who tramp the streets in their hard hats and work boots. Finally, after 50 years in the delta, the oil companies decided to install a proper electricity grid for local people and businesses.

Fillng up *A service station in Benin: a few bottles of fuel and a funnel.*

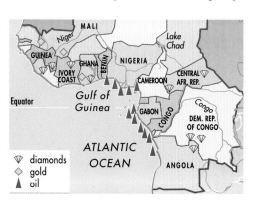

Blighted land Flames burn off excess fuel at oil installations in the polluted Niger delta.

When diamonds are deadly

Diamonds, exported both legally and illegally, are a vital source of foreign exchange for many African countries. They can also be a source of conflict. Control of the diamond fields is a prize in the civil wars which have ravaged Sierra Leone and Angola.

For the most part, the diamond mines of Central and West Africa are small-scale operations. The diamonds they produce are bought by large international groups, which are not always very scrupulous about checking whether the gems are legal or smuggled.

In the Central African Republic, diamonds are often found in riverbeds, having been washed down from their original lodging places. The country did not start exporting them on a large scale until independence from France. Nowadays, there is a thriving trade in contraband diamonds. European diamond-cutters confirm that every year they cut about a million carats (440 lb/200 kg) of diamonds from a country whose legal exports amount to no more than half that total. About 98 per cent of the country's legal exports come from nearly 80 000 miners, who sell their stones to around 160 official buyers. These in turn sell them on to two bureaus in the capital, Bangui.

Gems of war

Diamonds have played a key part in some of the region's bloodiest civil wars. Sierra Leone, with a population of nearly 5 million people, exports around 200 000 carats (88 lb/40 kg) of diamonds a year. During its civil war, however, the chief diamond-mining areas were controlled by the rebel Revolutionary United Front, notorious for terrorising civilians by chopping off their hands. The rebels used the diamond revenues to buy arms from neighbouring countries, such as Liberia. Thus the diamonds fuelled the civil war, and neither the rebels nor the countries profitably supplying them with arms had any great incentive to make peace.

In Angola, the long-standing civil war created a kind of economic partition. Anti-government UNITA rebels controlled the diamond-mining regions, while the government itself controlled the oil-producing regions. In the mid 1990s, UNITA was trading diamonds for arms at the rate of US$1 million's worth a day.

Purchasing power *A buyer in the Central African Republic. Diamonds represent half the country's exports.*

Water treasure *In the Central African Republic 'mining' often involves diving into river waters to gather the precious stones (left). Below: Workers search the muddy waters of a mine in Sierra Leone, where diamonds helped to prolong a bloody civil war.*

African gold

The Ashanti kings who once ruled Ghana sat on a stool that was covered in gold, and adorned themselves with golden necklaces, bracelets and anklets. Ghana, known in colonial times as the Gold Coast, is still a major source of the metal, along with Mali, Guinea and Burkina.

Panning for a fortune *Women in the gold fields of Guinea wash the gold-bearing sand in shallow bowls known as* batées.

The scene is like something out of a gold rush movie. The arid savannah spreads out on all sides, lonely and desolate, but around the mine all is frenzied activity. Prospectors dig pits and tunnels, hoping to find the nugget that will make their fortunes. Some, in their eagerness, neglect to shore up the roof and sides properly, and the tunnel collapses.

Family teamwork

Often the diggers work in family units. The father or uncle goes down into the pit, while the children stay at the top, hauling up the baskets of earth. They then tug the containers to a large heap, where other family members are stationed, sifting through the soil for the few precious specks of ore. Anything they find is carefully stored, often in an old aspirin bottle or the like. It is then sold on from middleman to middleman, until it reaches the government-owned gold buying office, the *Comptoir burkinabé des metaux precieux*, in Ouagadougou.

The middlemen include local buyers, who set themselves up in the villages that sprout in makeshift fashion around the major mining concessions. They buy the miners' lumps of ore, then melt and purify them. They are one element in a cast of characters drawn irresistibly to these settlements, and including smugglers, drugs dealers and would-be marabouts or holy men, who bless miners' pits for them or even claim to be able to detect hidden nuggets.

At the other end of the scale, major South African, Australian, American and Canadian mining companies all have stakes in the gold reserves of West Africa. As well as modernising existing operations, they are actively seeking out new or hitherto underexploited gold deposits and modernising existing operations. An example is the Novia Scotia-based company Etruscan Resources Inc, which is engaged in a number of exploration and mining projects. One of these is at Samira Hill in western Niger, where Etruscan is developing an open-pit gold mine in partnership with a Moroccan-owned company.

The Ghana-based Ashanti Goldfields Company is the most profitable mining company in Africa, employing 10 000 people in four countries – Ghana, Guinea, Tanzania and Zimbabwe – and quoted on both the London and New York stock exchanges. Modern Ghana, tenth in the world table of gold-producing nations, can still lay claim to being a golden coast.

In the scales *A dealer weighs gold at Dossui in Burkina (above). Left: A mud-caked miner holds out a few nuggets at Koma Bangou in Niger. He and his fellows risk life and limb in the hope of becoming rich men.*

Rare metals and minerals

Metals used in industry, such as tungsten and molybdenum, command high prices, and sub-Saharan Africa bears rich seams of them. The difficulties lie in their location and in the cost of setting up plants and transporting the ores to their far-off markets.

Burkina has large deposits of zinc, copper, marble and bauxite – all of them highly valuable commodities. But to a large extent, they lie there unexploited. The cost of building roads and railways to get access to them is prohibitive. One success story is at Tambao in the far north-east of the country, where the reserves of manganese are estimated at around 10 million tons. To encourage investment, the government built a special railway across 190 miles (300 km) of bush.

Guinea has a similar problem. Its bauxite reserves are colossal – estimated at around 2 billion tons – but little is mined because they are so remote.

Untapped reserves

During the 1970s and 1980s, uranium accounted for up to 80 per cent of Niger's exports. Aware of its overdependence, the government sought to develop the country's coal and gypsum reserves. They had some success, but further discoveries of iron, phosphates, copper, molybdenum, titanium and vanadium have had disappointing results, for the climate and the costs of access make international companies reluctant to invest.

Gabon is another important exporter of uranium, though the industry was a long time in developing. Exploration began in 1948, but it was seven years before the first deposits were found in 1955, and it took a few years more for the mines to become operational.

Profitable earth *Niger's uranium mines have created a bleak lunar landscape, but the profits for government revenues are enormous.*

As in Niger, the uranium ore is processed on the spot, which helps to reduce transport costs. Concentrated uranium is easier and cheaper to move by road and even air to Gabon's principal markets in France, Japan and Spain.

Wealth from the ground *A uranium processing plant in Gabon (above). The biggest buyer of Gabonese uranium is the French Atomic Energy Commission. It is mined around Moanda in the east of the country. Left: A sulphur mine in Senegal.*

CHAPTER 5

GROWING PAINS FOR AFRICA'S NEW NATIONS

The wind of change that swept through Africa in the 1960s gave hope to millions. With colonial rule consigned to history, new nations could build a better tomorrow for both present and unborn generations. But all too often, those hopes were dashed. In many countries, democracy has been painfully slow to emerge. Instead, dictators have taken power away from the people, squandered national wealth on self-aggrandising schemes, and often built up their own bank accounts. Central and West Africa is a complex tangle of ethnic groups, and violence has sometimes erupted between them. Chad, for instance, has endured civil wars since independence, the Democratic Republic of Congo is torn apart by conflict, and Nigeria's civil war in the 1960s caused 1.5 million deaths. Yet problems are being resolved. Today, countries such as Senegal, Guinea and Benin point the way to the future.

Carrying tomorrow's hopes: children in the Angolan capital, Luanda.

Carrying the catch Fishermen in Mbour, a large port south of Dakar.

Senegal: between sea and savannah

Stretching from the Atlantic coast to the high, sun-scorched savannahs of the Sahel, Senegal was the first of France's African colonies. And, following independence, it remains the most French of them all. Dakar, the capital, with its smart shops, pavement cafés and intellectual buzz, is a taste of Paris in the tropics.

S preading along the southern edge of the Cap Vert peninsula, Dakar hums with activity around its central Sandaga market. In the profusion of colour, the bright hues of the loose, kaftan-like garments known as boubous, worn by both sexes, stand out. Its street traders are among the most persistent in Africa. Tourists can find them next to impossible to shake off as they try to sell anything from sunglasses to tickets to a pop concert.

Only 8 miles (13 km) from Dakar lies Almadies Point, the westernmost point of continental Africa. Another excursion is to the island of Gorée, today an enchantment of colourwashed houses, but once a staging post in the slave trade. North of the capital, dunes line the Côte Sauvage (wild coast), battered by winds and ocean currents. South of the Cap Vert peninsula, the Petite Côte (little coast) enjoys a pleasant climate where temperatures range between 20° and 28°C (68° and 82°F). Long sandy beaches spread along the edges of its sheltered inlets.

The powerful brotherhoods

Inland, the barren expanses of the Sahel, covering the bulk of the country, are the heartlands of a very Senegalese version of Islam. Women are not required to wear the veil, and among the Wolof, the country's largest ethnic group, animist traditions survive alongside minarets and daily prayers to Allah. The main street in a Wolof village is always crooked: to build it straight would be to invite malicious spirits to take up residence. Some 90 per cent of Senegalese are Muslim, and their associations, known as brotherhoods, wield immense influence. The most powerful of these is the Mouride brotherhood, which stresses the sanctity of manual labour. Some of its members are even excused from fasting during the holy month of Ramadan, so long as they make up for it by working. The Great Mosque in their holy city, Touba, just under 100 miles (160 km) to the east of Dakar, is the burial place of Sheikh Amadou Bamba, who founded the brotherhood in 1895.

Holy bustle All is bustle and colour in Touba, the holy city of the Mouride brotherhood. Every year thousands of Mourides converge on the city during the Grand Magal festival to pray.

River border The Sénégal river marks the frontier with Mauritania.

Christians account for around 7 per cent of the population and are mostly confined to Dakar and the Petite Côte. In the forested south, most people hold fast to traditional animist beliefs. This includes the region of Casamance, which is largely cut off from the rest of the country by the sliver of The Gambia.

In Senegal, as in most of Africa, music plays a part in all the major events and festivities of life. Instruments include the *tana* or armpit drum. Shaped like an hourglass, it has iguana skins stretched across each end, with strings running between them. The player holds the instrument under his armpit, and by adjusting the pressure on the strings, he makes the iguana-skin heads tauter or slacker, changing the tone of the drum. The slit drum is made from a tree trunk that has been hollowed out through a slit. The *kora* is a 16-string harp, and the *balafon* a kind of xylophone, with keys made from wood and calabash.

The Gambia: frontiers created by colonialism

Pointing like a finger into the heart of Africa, The Gambia is a narrow ribbon of land on either side of the river from which it takes its name. This former British colony is a poor country, with an economy that depends on tourism and groundnuts.

The money-changer *A bureau de change in Banjul.*

Just 25 miles (40 km) wide and 200 miles (322 km) long, The Gambia is the perfect example of an African country that owes its existence to European rivalries. In the 17th and 18th centuries the British and French competed along the coast for the ivory, ebony, gold and slaves of the interior. The British had a fort and trading station on James Island, at the mouth of the Gambia river, while the French outpost was on nearby Albreda. Six times they attempted to capture the British fort, but each time they were repulsed. A treaty signed in 1783 allotted trading rights on the Gambia river to Britain, and France turned its attention to Senegal. In 1889 the two governments reached an agreement defining the current border between The Gambia and Senegal.

The Gambia, while relatively short, is also one of the most navigable rivers in Africa. The Scottish surgeon-explorer Mungo Park used it in 1795, and again in 1805 as his route into the African interior during his expeditions to trace the course of the Niger.

Chasing the slave ships

The British outlawed the slave trade in their empire in 1807, and nine years later built the fort of Bathurst on another island at the mouth of the river, as a base from which to hunt down slave ships and free their wretched cargoes. Bathurst, which eventually became the country's capital, was renamed Banjul on The Gambia's independence in 1965. Its cricket ground and ornamental cannon are relics of the days of British rule.

Sorting the catch   Fish is a staple in the diet of the Gambians, the majority of whom live near the sea or beside the river.

The Gambia is all but surrounded by its more prosperous neighbour, Senegal, but attempts to unite the two countries have foundered on the rock of the Gambians' refusal to give up their language and way of life. A loose confederation was set up in 1982, but it lasted only seven years.

Since Banjul is on an island, there is no room for it to expand. As a result, new towns have mushroomed on the Atlantic coast – places such as Serekunda, near Banjul, and Bakau, 6 miles (10 km) to the west. Built along beachfronts, where sea breezes temper the heat, these more modern towns have developed as resorts, with luxury hotels and restaurants. Visitors who venture inland along the river have the chance of seeing mangrove swamps, gallery forest, chimpanzees, leopards, elands and colourful migratory birds.

Cape Verde: the peril in blue seas

Spectacular mountains, dazzlingly white sands, blue seas and skies that are even bluer … the remote Cape Verde islands seem created to be a tropical paradise. But there is a threat in those cloudless skies: droughts have killed hundreds of thousands of islanders.

All in the family *Fishing in the waters around Cape Verde is still a small-scale family business.*

In 1456, Alvise Ca' da Mosto, a Venetian in the service of the Portuguese, was the first European to reach Cape Verde. The islands, he noted, 'seemed to be inhabited only by multitudes of pigeons.' The birds 'allowed themselves to be picked up, so ignorant were they of the danger represented by mankind.'

Portuguese peasants arrived six years later, to farm in this group of ten large islands and five islets, lying some 400 miles (645 km) off the coast of West Africa. At that time there was at least enough ground vegetation to justify the name *verde* ('green'). But the settlers cut down trees and their goats ate the grass. The naturalist Charles Darwin, who visited Cape Verde in the 19th century, described it as 'an utterly sterile land.'

Refugees from the Inquisition

The settlers founded Ribeiro Grande on São Tiago island, the first European city to be built in the tropics, and one that grew rich from the slave trade. Its wealth attracted the unwelcome attentions of pirates and other marauders – among them Sir Francis Drake, who raided it in 1585. As well as peasants in search of a better life, the founding settlers included Jewish refugees, fleeing the Inquisition. African slaves were brought in to work sugar and cotton plantations, and the different groups mingled to create today's predominantly mixed-race population.

The islanders have two languages: Portuguese for official communications and Crioulo, a dialect mixing archaic Portuguese and African words.

Drought and famine have been constant perils. One drought lasting from 1830 to 1833 resulted in the deaths of 30 000 people. The decline of the slave trade from the mid 19th century, combined with further droughts, sent waves of islanders emigrating to the African mainland and later to Portugal. The cycle of drought and emigration continued in the 20th century, during the course of which at least 75 000 died from famine. Today, more people of Cape Verde origin live outside the country than inside it. With their striking mountain scenery and sparkling offshore waters, the islands have tourist potential, but they remain grindingly poor and heavily reliant on foreign aid.

The capital is Praia on São Tiago, but one of the most attractive towns is Mindelo on São Vicente. It lines the edge of a bay, with mountains rising behind and houses climbing up them. The heart of the town is Cabral Square, where at weekends a band plays and people come to stroll and greet their friends. Cobbled streets lead down to the harbour, where women sit on doorsteps smoking pipes, while men sit at tables, gambling or playing chess. Stalls selling vegetables, sweets and tobacco line the streets. The pace of activity quickens when one of the ferries that ply between the islands is due in. People gather on the quayside, for there are goods to despatch and there may be friends to meet – or even newcomers.

The grin *A young mixed-race islander.*

Cape Verde

Homes with a view *As well as its old Portuguese charm, Fontainhas has a spectacular setting, perched on a barren escarpment on the island of Santo Antão.*

Mali: where cities are built of earth

Vast trading empires once prospered among the sands and savannahs of Mali. Today, it is one of the poorest countries in the world.

Headgear *Fulani women walk towards the market at Djenné.*

Caravans laden with salt still come down from the desert to the north, as they have done for well over 1000 years, though the camel trains are nothing like as impressive as they once were. On the banks of the Niger, they encounter traders who have paddled upriver in dugout pirogue canoes. They exchange salt for forest produce, such as cola nuts, the caffeine-rich seeds people chew as a stimulant or as an aid to digestion. Along the river banks, farmers grow the small-grained African rice in paddies inundated during the Niger's twice-yearly floods. In the savannah to the south, the key crop, pearl millet, has to be planted laboriously, seed by seed, in the bone-dry earth.

The romance of Timbuktu

In the south of Mali, among the myriad waterways where the Niger loses itself in its inland delta, a succession of empires flourished on the trade in salt, gold, tin, ivory and slaves between the different regions. Cities such as Timbuktu – in the Middle Ages one of the greatest centres of learning in the entire Muslim world – preserve something of their ancient aura of mystery and romance. Many of Timbuktu's banco (mudbrick) buildings have been restored,

presenting stoutly buttressed walls to the outside world, their heavy doors reinforced with huge nails.

According to a local saying, 'Timbuktu would be nothing without Djenné.' Another great mudbrick city, Djenné was built on an island in the Bani river, a tributary of the Niger. Like so many cities in the region, it prospered as a marketplace for the goods of desert, savannah and forest. Its narrow streets are flanked by two-storey houses, which are built and maintained by the members of a guild of masons, each of whom is allowed only one trowel. In the centre of the city, the streets emerge into an open square, where a market is held every Monday. On one side, Djenné's mosque rises, mud-baked and bristling with wooden beams in the style that has become a signature for the region – copied in the mosques of Ségou, San, Gao and many smaller communities.

The potter's tent *Pots dry in the sun outside a Tuareg tent pitched on the banks of the Niger at Gao (left). The tent itself is made from matting. Below: Amid the surrounding dunes, a few scrubby trees grow in the gardens of a desert settlement.*

Forests and islands of Guinea-Bissau

Sandwiched between Senegal and Guinea, the former Portuguese colony of Guinea-Bissau has considerable potential for growth. But first it has to recover from a legacy of misrule, and to heal the scars of civil war.

Three large rivers, the Geba, Grande and Cacine, meander across the steaming lowlands of Guinea-Bissau, creating highways into the interior. Mangrove swamps spread along the country's deeply indented coastline, and offshore lie tropical islands. This is a land of stunning scenery, with promising reserves of timber, phosphates, bauxite and oil. Yet it is also an impoverished land, for its economy has been stunted by a century of colonial misrule and by military coups and civil wars since it won independence.

The long war for liberty

In the Middle Ages, Guinea-Bissau was a kingdom within the empire of Mali. Its people, the Gabu, lived by growing rice and trading sea salt with peoples to the east. From the 15th century onwards, the Portuguese exported slaves from the region, but did not seek to impose colonial rule until the 1880s, during the 'Scramble for Africa'.

Open-air schooling *Classrooms are make-shift affairs, particularly on the islands of the Bijagós Archipelago.*

Hunting and fishing *The forests abound in small game, and the swamps in fish and shrimps, one of the country's chief exports.*

In the 1960s, Portugal's dictator, Antonio Salazar, refused to bend to the wind of change sweeping through Africa, and independence came only in 1974, after a 13-year guerrilla war, led by the Marxist Amilcar Cabral. The country was riven by civil war in the 1990s. President Joao Viera, who came to power through an army coup, was deposed in another coup in 1999, as was his successor, President Kumba Yala in 2003. The military leader General Verissimo Correia Seabra took control of the country at that point.

The country's capital, Bissau, standing on the banks of the Geba river, preserves many fine buildings from the Portuguese era. Forests stretch inland, while offshore lie the 15 main islands and countless islets of the Bijagós Archipelago. Poincianas poke their heads above surrounding trees in the island forests, glowing in season with fiery red blossoms. Mangrove swamps and sandy beaches line the shores. Palm products are the islands' chief exports.

Their people are the Bidyogo, animists who make elaborate masks for the dances and other ceremonies that accompany such rites of passage as marriage, burial or the initiation of boys into manhood. They also make statuettes to represent their ancestors. Both masks and statuettes are painted in much brighter colours than those

Guinea: the long, hard road to democracy

Guinea was once one of the most prosperous countries in West Africa, and it is still one of the most beautiful. But after its leader rejected an offer to remain within the French-African community, France left the new nation to fend for itself and President Sékou Touré turned out to be better at delivering oppression than prosperity.

Highland hairdos *A Fulani 'beauty parlour' in the Fouta Djallon.*

When President de Gaulle offered France's West African colonies internal self-government in 1958, the Guinean leader, Sékou Touré, surprised the world by saying no. Only full independence would do: he preferred 'poverty in liberty to wealth in slavery'. The country became independent in October of that year, with Sékou Touré as president.

Marxist experiment

De Gaulle immediately cut off all French support, and the country's

Food preparation *Pounding millet in a Guinea village.*

economy was severely damaged. An unpromising start was made even worse by Touré's attempts to force Guinea into a Soviet-style mould. He jailed, tortured, exiled or executed opponents. He turned to the Soviet Union for economic aid, though the benefits were often questionable – on one occasion a consignment of snow ploughs was delivered instead of tractors. Sometimes lambasting the West, sometimes the Soviets, he played off both sides against each other during the Cold War.

His regime was unpopular, but he survived a number of attempts to oust him, including an invasion by exiles, backed up by Portuguese troops from Guinea-Bissau, in 1970. The highly centralised economy suffered, however. By the time of his death in 1984, a country whose agriculture had once been among the most prosperous in the region was unable to feed itself. Not even its considerable mineral riches in diamonds, gold and a quarter of the world's known bauxite reserve could keep it afloat.

Sékou Touré's successor, Colonel Lansana Conté, seemed to offer greater democracy, freeing political prisoners and encouraging exiles to

return. In fact, it was 1993 before the first multiparty presidential election was held – won by Conté. Guinea's constitution allowed a president only two terms of office, but Conté organised a referendum to sidestep that rule. Many voters saw him as a figure of stability in a region racked by its opposite. In the late 1990s, Guinea's problems were compounded when the civil wars in neighbouring Sierra Leone and Liberia spilled over the frontier, bringing floods of refugees.

Given political stability, Guinea has great economic and tourist potential. Sandy beaches and mangrove swamps, rich in wildlife, spread along the coast. Inland, rise the highlands of the Fouta Djallon, where three great rivers, the Niger, Sénégal and Gambia, have their headwaters, and Fulani herders graze their cattle on green pastures. Along the border with the modern state of Mali is where the great medieval empire of Mali was born. Beneath the forested flanks of the Nimba range, in the far south, lie some of the region's richest seams of iron ore.

Evening calm *Night falls over one of the enchanting beaches that line the coast of Guinea.*

Sierra Leone and Liberia: founded in the name of freedom

Both Sierra Leone and Liberia were founded as colonies where free and runaway slaves from the New World could return to Africa and live as free men and women. But what began in idealism foundered in class and ethnic conflicts, and slid into civil war.

The lucky ones *These children, in a transit camp in Sierra Leone, escaped being forced to join rebel militias.*

When British antislavery campaigners founded Freetown – now Sierra Leone's capital – in 1787, the slave trade and slavery were still in full swing in the British Empire. The settlement on a stretch of coast not yet claimed by any European power was a private philanthropic venture, which only became a crown colony after Britain abolished its slave trade in 1807. Liberia was a larger-scale operation, founded by American abolitionists for freed slaves in the 1820s. It became an independent republic – Africa's first – in 1847, with a constitution based on that of the United States.

In both countries, the freed slaves established themselves as local elites, who kept a tight hold on economic and political power. In Liberia, the so-called Americo-Liberians set up a plantation economy and lived in houses similar to those of the American South. The country's indigenous Africans were an underclass, allowed only the most menial employment.

By the 1960s, discontent was mounting as neighbouring countries won their independence. When President William Tubman died in 1971, after a 27-year rule, his successor, William Tolbert, attempted modest reforms. But these failed to satisfy the opposition. Finally, in 1980, the former underclass ended the hegemony of the Americo-Liberians: Tolbert was killed in a coup led by Master Sergeant Samuel Doe. The new balance of power did not bring peace, however. By the end of the decade, tension had slipped into civil war, with rival warlords financing themselves from the sale of contraband diamonds and rubber. In 2003, however, the peace process began after President Charles Taylor was forced into exile by rebels, following accusations of supporting those in Sierra Leone responsible for widescale atrocities.

Pulling back from the brink

In Sierra Leone, the descendants of the freed slaves are called Creoles. At the time of the country's independence from Britain in 1962, its leader was a Creole, Sir Milton Margai. Political instability took hold five years later, when the civilian government of Siaka Stevens was overthrown in a coup. Another coup restored Stevens to power, and in 1978 he declared Sierra Leone a one-party state. In the 1990s, the civil war in Liberia spread to Sierra Leone, centring itself in the southern, diamond-producing region of the country.

Here, however, international intervention eventually succeeded. United Nations and British forces imposed a ceasefire and started disarming the rebels. In January 2002 the disarmament process was declared complete. In May the Sierra Leone People's Party of President Ahmad Tejan Kabbah won a landslide victory in parliamentary elections.

Stolen childhood *Children in Liberia are seen as part of the work force.*

Ready to wed *Two Liberian women, painted and made up for a traditional wedding.*

Diamond mine *A key war aim for both sides in Sierra Leone was control of the diamond fields.*

Burkina: 'land of honest people'

In the 1980s, the reforming president Thomas Sankara changed his country's name from Upper Volta to Burkina Faso – 'land of honest people'. He gave it a new flag and a new national anthem, but he could not give it new land. Years of overgrazing, and the fierce African sun, have turned much of Burkina into a dust bowl.

Seventy different languages are spoken in Burkina Faso. Chief among them is French, the language of the former colonial power. Moré is the language of the majority Mossi people; and Dyula is the language of the Dyula people, who are renowned traders. Scenery ranges from the dunes of Oursi in the north-east to the sandstone plateaus of the south-west, fringed by the cliffs of the Banfora Escarpment.

Sculpture festival

Human creativity is expressed in the rock paintings of Aribinda, the tombs of the Mossi kings at Komtoega and the majestic contemporary sculptures at Laongo, north-east

Wealth of the wanderers Like all nomads, the Fulani herders who roam the north of Burkina carry their riches in the form of ornaments.

of the capital Ouagadougou. These granite bas-reliefs are the work of local sculptors who gather in Laongo every February for a festival of stone carving.

In Burkina the arts are actively promoted. For ten days in February and March every other year, Ouagadougou hosts an African film and television festival, the biggest cultural event in Africa, bringing thousands of visitors to the capital. Other arts events in Ouagadougou include an International Crafts Salon, a National Culture Week and a theatre and puppet festival – all of which draw entrants and visitors from well beyond Burkina.

Different ethnic groups have always lived side by side here, and the importance of cooperation is emphasised in the country's myths and legends. Many of these involve the warrior-princess Yennega. The daughter of a Mossi king, she succeeded, where male

warriors had failed, in bringing his enemies, the awe-inspiring Nioniosse people, to heel. On another occasion, her horse bolted and she was rescued by a prince of the Mande people. They fell in love and had a son, whom they called Ouedraogo – meaning 'stallion'.

A succession of coups

Since winning independence from France in 1960, Burkina has suffered frequent coups. The military deposed the authoritarian president Maurice Yaméogo in 1966, but were unable to solve the country's basic problem – impoverishment of both the people and the soil. Within living memory, the central plateau of Mossi was forested; today, trees are a rarity there.

In 1983, the fifth coup in 17 years brought the charismatic Captain Thomas Sankara to power. He set up vaccination and housing projects, had trees planted to try to stop soil erosion and supported women's rights. To combat corruption, he decreed that ministers and officials, including himself, should make public the details of their bank accounts. Thomas Sankara was shot dead in 1987, during yet another army coup. His successor, Blaise Compaoré, introduced limited democratic reforms, but his human rights record in office has caused concern. The closing of the country's biggest gold mine, in 1999, has compounded his problems.

Council meeting A Mossi chief presides over his council of advisers.

Built for defence The Gurunsi people in the Pô region of southern Burkina live in fortified mud-brick houses.

109

Ivory Coast: fallen idol of West Africa

Under the autocratic rule of the 'father of the nation', Félix Houphouët-Boigny, Ivory Coast was a model of political stability and prosperity. In recent years, however, fluctuating world commodity prices have brought leaner times, and underlying tensions have come to the surface.

Full regalia   *An Akan chief in Bondoukou.*

For more than three decades, Ivory Coast was spared the instability and violence that afflicted so many of its neighbours. Its first president, Félix Houphouët-Boigny, came from a family of Baule tribal chiefs in the centre of the country, and was aware of the differences between the inhabitants of the savannahs of the Muslim north and those of the forests and cocoa and coffee plantations of the Christian south. The French colonial authorities had favoured the southern Christians, and many of these moved into key posts under Houphouët-Boigny. But he was also careful to maintain the balance between different communities. For example, he promoted the cultivation of cotton in the north and built the great Kossou Dam in the centre of the country. Ivory Coast has a large population of Muslim immigrants from Burkina (currently 4 million out of a total population of 16 million), who originally came to work on the plantations. Proclaiming that the 'land belongs to those who cultivate it', Houphouët-Boigny gave them the right to buy land and become farmers in their turn. Not surprisingly, they tended to be loyal supporters of his regime.

A village transformed

Houphouët-Boigny held together a country containing more than 60 ethnic groups, and more than 200 religious sects, ranging from hyper-strict Wahabi Muslims to Harristes – followers of the Protestant preacher and former sailor William Wadé Harris. The president's birthplace, the village of Yamoussoukro, was completely transformed after he declared it the country's official capital, in 1983. The Basilica of Nôtre Dame de la Paix, closely modelled on St Peter's, Rome, was built in three years. The Presidential Palace holds the tomb of Houphouët-Boigny, who died in 1993.

If the president poured money into the village of his birth, so too, while he was alive, did France pour money and expertise into Ivory Coast. During the 1960s and 1970s, its economy grew at a rate of 6 to 7 per cent a year. Ivory Coast's chief exports are cocoa and coffee, and world prices for both these commodities were high and stable. At the same time, unlike many of his counterparts in the region, Houphouët-Boigny followed a pro-Western line, and Western governments responded with generous aid packages. The government had ample revenues to distribute among the regions, to build roads and schools and to pay the salaries of its civil servants – who sent money back to their villages.

Good times end

The boom came to an end in the 1980s, however, with tumbling world prices for cocoa and coffee. At first, the government sought to shore up farmers' incomes by buying their crops at

Keeping up the style   *Malinke immigrants from Niger have settled in the Odienné region, building villages in their traditional style.*

110

special prices, but this policy had to be abandoned under pressure from the all-powerful international financial institutions. In the years of its prosperity, the government had borrowed heavily abroad in order to pay for development projects. It found itself with a large foreign debt, which it had increasing difficulty in repaying. The population was growing fast; so were poverty and unemployment.

When Houphouët-Boigny died, he was succeeded peacefully by the President of the National Assembly, Henri Konan Bédié. But discontent was growing, much of it directed against the Muslim immigrants from Burkina. Bédié himself encouraged the nationalist fervour, partly to divert attention from the country's economic problems, partly to make trouble for his rival, the Muslim Alassane Ouattara. In December 1999, Robert Gueï ousted Bédié in Ivory Coast's only successful military coup.

New and old   Modern tower blocks loom over the market in the Plateau district of Abidjan.

Christians versus Muslims

Gueï then held presidential elections, which he claimed to have won. But there were widespread allegations of vote-rigging, and demonstrators poured into the streets in support of Laurent Gbagho, leader of the left-wing Ivorian Popular Front. Gueï fled and Gbagho proclaimed himself president. There was no proof, however, that Gbagho had been the real winner of the elections, and Ouattara called for a fresh vote. The country's ethnic and religious faultlines came savagely to the surface when fighting broke out between Gbagho's supporters, mainly Christians from the south, and those of Ouattara, who were mainly Muslims from the north. According to official figures, 171 people died in the violence. After suppressing an attempted coup in January 2000, Gbagho sought reconciliation with his political opponents. But his regime has been widely criticised for human rights abuses, including the use of torture against opponents. There have also been allegations that child slaves are used to work in the plantations.

'Electricity in every village'

One of Félix Houphouët-Boigny's ambitions for his country was that there should be 'electricity in every village'. When the Kossou Dam was completed in 1972, it went a long way towards achieving that goal, doubling the country's electricity production. The 5000 ft (1500 m) dam was built across the Bandama Blanc river, creating a reservoir with a surface area of 656 sq miles (1700 km²).

The reservoir is also a source of irrigation, enabling more crops to be grown in the savannah region. And it was stocked with fish to provide local people with an extra source of food and income. On the negative side, thousands of farmers were displaced from land in the flooded valley, and rain forest was cleared at the southern end.

Rock-strewn water highway
Three great rivers flow through Ivory Coast: the Sassandra, the Bandama and the Comoé (left).

Ghana: years of hope and crisis

The British colony of the Gold Coast was the first black African country to win full independence from an imperial power. A new name was needed for the new nation, and its first leader, Kwame Nkrumah, decided that none was more fitting than that of one of the great empires of medieval Africa – Ghana.

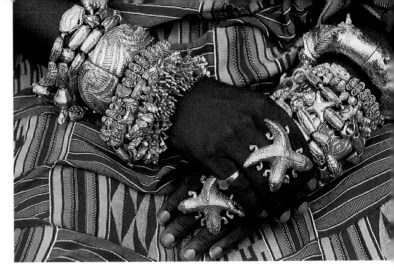

Gold for sovereignty   *A modern gold watch peeps out among the traditional gold bracelets worn by the late Ashanti king, Opoku Ware II, for the 25th anniversary of his reign in 1995.*

Within a few years of its independence, in 1957, Ghana had become symbolic both of the hopes of African nationalists and of their tragic disappointments. Nkrumah became president when the country proclaimed itself a republic in 1960, then president for life when he declared it a one-party state in 1964. But his overambitious plans led to economic crisis, despite the country's rich resources of gold, bauxite, manganese and diamonds, and its position as a leading exporter of cocoa. Nkrumah's primary concern, it seemed, was to cut a figure in the world. He built up his personal bodyguard to the size of a regiment, and spent large sums on building projects. There were food shortages, and in 1966, while on a visit to China, Nkrumah was ousted in a military coup.

Rawlings takes charge

The country remained in crisis, with a succession of coups bringing corrupt and frequently incompetent leaders to power. After a coup led by Flight Lieutenant Jerry Rawlings in 1979 two of these former presidents, Colonel Ignatius Acheampong and General

All in red   *Huge crowds gathered for the funeral of Opoku Ware II in 1999.*

Frederick Akuffo, were tried and executed for embezzlement. Rawlings then handed power to an elected president. But with the economy still stagnating, he took charge again in 1981, and put the country on a steadier footing by slashing the bureaucracy, devaluing the currency and securing loans from the World Bank and International Monetary Fund. After re-election in 1996, he stood down for the 2000 election, which was won by an Oxford-educated lawyer, John Kufuor.

Ashanti power

The valley and basin of the Volta dominate Ghana geographically. But it is the gold reserves of the forested central region that have been the key to much of the country's history. Akan people arriving from the east established the first kingdoms in the 13th century. Later immigrants, coming down the Volta valley from the north, grew rich from the trade in forest gold and forest-grown cola nuts – valued as a stimulant and an aid to digestion. In the late 17th century, an Ashanti chief, Osei Tutu, united the various branches of his nation to create the Ashanti kingdom, which remained the dominant power in the south until the 19th century.

It was gold, meanwhile, that had first drawn European traders and seafarers to this portion of the Guinea Coast. In 1482, the Portuguese established a fort at Elmina – São Jorge da Mina (Saint George of the Mine) – to the west of modern Cape Coast. In the end, though, it was the 'black gold' of slavery that made the European traders rich. The slave trade was also the key to Ashanti power: the Ashanti kings sold slaves to the Europeans in return for firearms, which they used to maintain their supremacy in the interior.

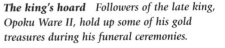

The king's hoard   *Followers of the late king, Opoku Ware II, hold up some of his gold treasures during his funeral ceremonies.*

Togo: West Africa in miniature

A sliver of a country, squeezed between Ghana and Benin, Togo still manages to pack in just about every type of landscape to be found in West Africa, apart from sun-baked deserts.

Market force *Political and economic instability in the early 1990s dented the prosperity of Togo's famous* **nana Benz**, *market women, specialising in textiles.*

More than 30 different ethnic groups live in Togo, each with its own language and customs. The country measures only 335 miles (540 km) from north to south and 35 miles (50 km) across. Yet its scenery ranges from lagoons and sandy beaches along the coast to hills and rain forests in the south west and open savannah grasslands on the plateaus to the north.

Its ethnic diversity has created a rich crafts heritage. Around Tchamba in the centre, a tradition has developed of engraving calabashes with intricate geometric patterns. The people of the north-east use heated tools to burn designs onto wood and other materials. The Bassari are famed for their skills as blacksmiths, and the Kotokoli are equally admired as weavers. The Ewé are master carvers, who will sculpt a single block of mahogany, ebony or teak into a table, chair or a strange human figure.

A sporting spectacular

The ancestors of the Ewé arrived from Nigeria in the 14th to 16th centuries, and today they form Togo's largest ethnic group. The dominant group in the north of the country are the Kabyé, who every year stage one of the greatest sporting spectacles of Africa. During the nine days of the Evala all-in wrestling championships, hundreds of young men test their courage, strength and skill. In former centuries, the Kabyé sold slaves to the Mina people of the coast, who then sold them on to European slavers.

For a long time, Togo was a buffer zone between the African kingdoms of Ashanti to the west and Dahomey to the east. It became a German protectorate during the 'Scramble for Africa' of the 1880s, but was taken over by British and French forces in August 1914 – the first Allied victory of the First World War. The western British slice was eventually incorporated into the Gold Coast (later Ghana) and the eastern French sector won independence as Togo in 1960. Its first president, Sylvanus Olympio, was killed in a coup in 1963, and his successor was ousted four years later by Sergeant Gnsassingbe Eyadéma (now General Eyadéma).

One of Eyadéma's first acts was to ban opposition political parties – a ban that was lifted under French pressure in 1991. His regime has been accused of human rights violations, rigging elections and selling arms to Angola's UNITA rebels in return for diamonds. Amnesty International reported that hundreds of opposition supporters were killed in the 1998 presidential election campaign.

Laid out to dry *Fishermen along Togo's short coastline mending and drying their nets.*

Home defence *Stout walls defend the homes of the Somba people in northern Togo, recalling the time when villagers had to defend themselves against raids by slave-hunters.*

Benin: where voodoo outlives Marxism

The powerful kingdom of Dahomey grew rich from supplying slaves to Europeans. Now renamed Benin, it presents a cultural mix that contains an intriguing dash of bygone Europe.

Cheerful task *Preparing spicy fish – a favourite dish in Benin.*

Benin became a French colony in the 1880s, and its chief port and unofficial capital, Cotonou, is so strongly influenced by French culture that it has been called the 'Latin Quarter of Africa'. The official capital, Porto-Novo, owes more to Portuguese adventurers of the 16th century – even its name, bestowed because the landscape reminded them of home.

The Portuguese were prominent, too, in Ouidah, former chief port of the kingdom of Dahomey. In 1818, Francisco Felix de Souza backed a revolt that placed a new king on Dahomey's throne. As a reward he was made Viceroy of Ouidah. The port shipped out slaves, chiefly to Brazil, and de Souza encouraged the development of a large Afro-Brazilian community, consisting of slave-traders and of freed slaves returning from Brazil. Today, this community still plays an

Quiet capital *Life is slow-paced on the streets of Porto-Novo, the political capital of Benin.*

important part in the city's life, and there is still a de Souza as Ouidah's hereditary viceroy.

The Fon kings of Dahomey were constantly at war, seeking prisoners to sell as slaves or to sacrifice, so that they would not lack for servants in the afterworld. Behind the 33 ft (10 m) high walls of their palace, in Abomey, they were protected by a women-only bodyguard – called the Amazons by Europeans.

When Christmas was abolished

Modern Benin is one of the poorest countries in the world, but by regional standards it has enjoyed relative stability. The first dozen years of independence saw a succession of coups, but in 1972 Major Mathieu Kérékou took charge. At first he followed a strongly Marxist-Leninist line, changing the country's name to the People's Republic of Benin, setting up collective farms and abolishing Christmas. But in 1989, with the economy collapsing and students and unpaid civil servants demonstrating on the streets, he renounced communism and started to liberalise the economy. He lost presidential elections in 1991, and handed over peacefully to the new president, Nicéphore Soglo. At the next election, in 1996, he was returned to power.

The strength of voodoo

Benin is the heartland of *vodoun*, the ancestral religion of the Fon people, with its charms, fetishes and worship of the *vodun* spirits. It was slaves from this part of Africa who took vodoun to Haiti, where it became voodoo. Kérékou disapproved of vodoun, and tried to ban it when he first came to power. Soglo, though a devout Catholic, who regularly went to Mass, lifted the ban, and instituted a national vodoun day – January 10. Vodoun remains entwined with everyday life – most Fon families have a relative who is a vodoun priest or priestess. And it does no harm for the popularity of politicians for them to be seen attending a vodoun ceremony.

Commercial capital *Cotonou's deep-water harbour, completed in 1965, has assured its position as Benin's chief port and economic capital.*

Niger: the struggle against poverty

The northern two-thirds of the Republic of Niger is a barren wilderness, merging into the Sahara, where only Tubu and Tuareg nomads live. The bulk of the population in this, the second-poorest country in the world, ekes out a living in a narrow south-western strip, along the course of the Niger river.

A folk saying sums how vital are Niger's two staple foods: 'With milk and millet, the child can grow and the man work.' Vegetables are grown in a few places, with some sorghum and rice along the banks of the Niger. And cotton and groundnuts grown for export had some success until the great drought of 1968-73. Wells ran dry, livestock died, crops withered. Today, Niger is the world's second-poorest country after Sierra Leone and depends heavily on international aid.

Life on less than a dollar a day

Niger has rich uranium deposits around Arlit in the north-west, and for a time it was the world's third-largest producer, and seemingly set for a mini-boom. The Chernobyl nuclear disaster of 1986 dashed the nation's hopes. Demand for uranium slumped, prices spiralled downwards and mining became uneconomic for companies faced with the high costs of transport in a landlocked country. Another mineral, gold, lures people to the Sirba river, in the far west. Armed with primitive panning equipment, men from

Face painting *A Tuareg woman. About a sixth of Niger's population are nomads.*

Urban sprawl *Mud houses in Tahoua, an important trading town on the road between Niamey and Agadez.*

Niger, Burkina and Mali sift through the river sediment. Any precious grains they find will be sold to Hausa traders at derisory prices. Even so, in a country where more than 60 per cent of people live off less than US$1 a day, small sums will help to stave off hunger for the family back in the village.

Since independence from France in 1960, coups and military rule have dominated politics. One president was murdered by his own bodyguard. Elections in 1999 were won by the reformer Tandja Mamadou.

War of the sands

On May 7, 1990, a group of armed Tuareg nomads attacked the sub-prefecture at Tchin-Tabaradene in Niger's western province of Tahoua. It marked the start of a five-year guerrilla war. At stake was a way of life. Traditionally free to wander across large parts of five modern states – Niger, Mali, Algeria, Libya and Burkina – the Tuareg had suffered from the restrictions of more tightly patrolled borders and the decline of the trans-Saharan caravan routes. Their allies in rebellion were their age-old enemies, the Tubu. The government, they claimed, had promised economic aid, but had failed to deliver it. A ceasefire was finally agreed with one rebel group, the Revolutionary Armed Forces of the Sahara, in 1995; the more hard-line Democratic Renewal Front made peace in 1997. The nomads won a measure of self-rule, but tensions remain.

Nigeria: Africa's unwieldy and troubled giant

Elected governments have a poor survival record in Nigeria. The most populous country in Africa, it has suffered the various torments of ethnic conflict, civil war, military coups, corruption and environmental pollution, often on a dramatic scale.

Listening to head office *Communications are primitive in much of Nigeria – but not for the oil companies.*

Nigeria is an unwieldy country to rule. Nearly five times the size of the United Kingdom, with a population of 120 million, it has more than 250 different ethnic groups.

The three largest are the Hausa-Fulani in the north, the Yoruba in the south-west and the Ibo in the south-east. The Hausa are mostly Muslims, with a strong warrior tradition. Hausa kingdoms have existed since the Middle Ages, and their emirs are still influential figures. The Yoruba are craftsmen and farmers, who are also, in cities such as Ife, heirs to a sophisticated urban tradition. The Ibo are farmers and traders. The south has a history of contacts with Europeans, dating back to the 16th century. Its people are mostly Christians or followers of animist religions. And it is generally richer than the north: its soil is more fertile, and it contains the country's all-important oil fields.

Northerner against southerner

Until 1960, Nigeria was a colony of Britain, and the British way of dealing with its size and diversity was to create a federation, dividing the country into three zones, each with its own prime minister and civil service, but also with a federal government and premier. Following independence, however, the federal system came under challenge. In 1966, the federal premier, the northerner Sir Abubakar Tafawa Balewa, was assassinated and General Johnson Ironsi, an

Prayer time *The thousand-year-old realm of Kano in the north is an important centre of Muslim learning.*

Fela Kuti, the wild voice of protest

Nobody, probably, has inspired more adoration among the ordinary people of Nigeria and more hatred among most of its rulers than the keyboard-player, saxophonist and singer Fela Kuti (1938-97). He was the inventor of Afro-beat, a blending of local styles with American jazz, blues and rock. In his hands, it was a music of protest, denouncing corruption and oppression. He was regularly beaten and jailed by the authorities, but the people loved him. Hundreds would wait for his arrival at The Shrine, his club in Lagos. He was also famous for his spectacular appetite for women and drugs – he once wed, in one day, all 27 female members of his band, only to divorce them, en masse, seven years later. When he died of AIDS, a million people turned out in the streets of Lagos for his funeral. His son Femi carries on his musical legacy.

Fishing frenzy *In the annual Argungu fishing festival, drummers in canoes drive fish towards nets in the shallows.*

Ibo, became head of state. His ambition to abolish the federation and impose central rule sent Hausa rioters rampaging through the streets and killing thousands of Ibo traders. In July, Ironsi himself was killed during a coup which brought a northerner, Lt Colonel Yakubu Gowon, to power. In May 1967, fearful of northern domination and bolstered by growing oil wealth from the wells of the Niger delta and offshore in the Bight of Biafra, they seceded. The result of this attempt to break away from the federation was a civil war in which nearly 1.5 million Biafrans were killed or died of starvation. Biafra surrendered to the Nigerian army in January 1970.

Paddle power Transporting oil drums in Lagos harbour. Nigeria exports crude oil but, lacking refineries, has to import petrol.

Tyranny and ecological disaster

The next 30 years saw eight changes of government, all but two of them as a result of coups. In 1983, the probable victor was Chief Moshood Abiola, but he never even got as far as the presidential palace, because the military annulled the results of the poll. Abiola died in custody. The country's reputation reached a low point under General Sani Abacha, who seized power in 1993. His regime suppressed protests by the Ogoni and other peoples of the Niger delta against the ecological devastation brought to their homeland by the operations of the oil industry. His army killed demonstrators and looted homes.

But what caused outrage around the world was the hanging, in November, 1995, of the playwright Ken Saro-Wiwa

and eight other leaders of the Ogoni struggle. Nigeria was suspended from membership of the Commonwealth because of the executions, and the European Union applied sanctions. When Abacha died, in 1998 of a heart attack, he was reputed to have amassed a personal fortune of US$10 billion.

His death opened the way for elections, which were held in 1999 and gave hope for a better future. For the winner was Olusegun Obasanjo, a former general who first came to power as the result of a coup in 1976, but three years later handed over peacefully to an elected president and retired to life as a pig farmer. Obasanjo stayed out of politics until convinced that he should return for the 1999 contest. He went on to win the elections held in 2003.

Conflicts over shariah law

The task facing the new president was immense. In the previous 20 years, Nigeria's standard of living had halved. Although the country is Africa's biggest oil-producing nation, the price of petrol was exorbitantly high because of a lack of refineries – some people took matters into their own hands by tapping directly into oil pipelines. In 2001, Nigeria was rated the second most corrupt country in the world, after Bangladesh. Ethnic tensions remained high. A number of northern states decided to impose Islamic shariah law, leading to conflicts with Christians living in the north, in which hundreds died. Some groups even started expressing separatist ambitions, reviving bitter memories of the Biafran war.

Nigeria's largest ethnic groups

NIGER

Niger

BENIN

Hausa-Fulani

Lake Chad

Abuja

Benue

Yoruba

Ibo

CAMEROON

Gulf of Guinea

In all their finery Religious festivals in the north recall the conversion of the region to Islam, often by the sword.

Chad: a land of potential riches paralysed by civil war

The people of Chad's northern deserts are predominantly Arab and Muslim; those of the southern grasslands mostly black and Christian. The resulting disunity has crippled progress.

During the 19th century, Arab kingdoms in the north of Chad prospered on the cross-Sahara trade in salt, copper, gold and, above all, slaves. Their cavalry and foot soldiers would descend on the villages of the black people of the south and rope them together for a forced march to the slave markets of the coast.

Libya steps in

Today, the country has the potential to be wealthy once again, for it has abundant mineral resources. But since winning independence from France in 1960, it has been cheated of this prize by four decades of civil war. The first president of independent Chad, N'Garta Tombalbaye, came from the country's largest ethnic group, the Sara of the south, and he lost little time in declaring opposition parties illegal. The Arabs of the north could not accept domination by a people their forefathers had enslaved, and Frolinat, the Front for the Liberation of Chad, launched a guerrilla campaign.

Tombalbaye, an authoritarian who made enemies even in the south, was killed in 1975, in a coup led by another southerner, General Félix Malloum. After Malloum was ousted in turn, in 1979, a northern-led coalition government took over. But the northern forces began to fragment, along tribal lines. The Libyan leader, Colonel Gaddafi,

saw in the confusion a chance both to help his fellow Arabs and to expand Libya's frontiers. He had supplied arms to Frolinat since 1971, and in 1980 he invaded the border area of Aouzou. Hissène Habré, whose power base lay among the Daza people of the northeast, called in French help to drive the Libyans and their allies out of most of the country. But his triumph did not last. A new Libyan-backed group, the Patriotic Salvation Front, captured the capital, N'Djamena, in 1990. Its leader, Idriss Déby, won Chad's first ever multiparty presidential elections in 1996. Peace was still elusive. Yet another northern rebel group arose, and fighting continued until Libya brokered a ceasefire in 2002.

During the fighting, Chad's immense mineral potential was largely neglected. The country has reserves of gold, uranium, bauxite, tin, tungsten, titanium, iron ore, natron, kaolin – and oil. In 2000, however, a consortium of oil companies started to develop fields around Doba in the south of the country. Another important resource, Lake Chad itself, presents a bleak picture. In the mid 1960s it covered 10 000 sq miles (26 000 km^2). Today, it has shrunk by 95 per cent, partly as a result of climate change and lower rainfall, partly because the countries sharing it – Chad, Niger, Nigeria and Cameroon – have drawn off too much water for irrigation.

Gateway to the Sahara *Foodsellers in Faya, an oasis in northernmost Chad.*

Lake in the desert *Waters from the Tibesti massif feed a lake in the far north.*

The long torment of the Central African Republic

The region that now makes up the Central African Republic was once a refuge for communities fleeing from Arab slave-raiders. In colonial days its people were forced at gunpoint to labour for their masters. As if these miseries were not enough, the country fell into the hands of the brutal 'Emperor' Jean-Bedel Bokassa.

The self-aggrandising antics of Jean-Bedel Bokassa thrust the Central African Republic into the headlines in the 1970s. Bokassa had seized power in a military coup in 1965. He later proclaimed himself president for life. Then, in 1977, this former mission-school pupil astonished the world by elevating himself to emperor – placing the crown on his head himself, in imitation of his hero, Napoleon. His 'reign' lasted only two more years, but they were years of horror. He gave diamonds to the wives of foreign politicians and diplomats – and cut the ears off men jailed for theft.

Massacre of the children

When schoolchildren demonstrated against being forced to buy uniforms made with cloth from a factory owned by his wife, his troops massacred 100 of them. This time the 'emperor' had gone too far. In 1979, France sent commandos to overthrow him and restore the president he had ousted in 1965, David Dacko.

Historically, the plateau of the Central African Republic has been a place of refuge. Among its earliest inhabitants were the Babinga, a Pygmy people, traditionally living as hunter-gatherers in the forests, though many today are adopting a more settled way of life. The bulk of the population arrived in the 18th and 19th centuries. They came from the north and east and were fleeing raids by Arab slave-traders. In the 1880s the French established a base on the Ubangi river which eventually became the capital, Bangui.

The right to grow cotton, coffee and tobacco was farmed out to private companies, whose harsh treatment of their African workers caused an outcry in France. The colony, Ubangi-Shari, was made part of French Equatorial Africa in 1910, and became a prime destination for big game hunters. Nowadays, its rain forests are among the last surviving refuges of the lowland gorilla and forest elephant. Its mineral riches include substantial reserves of diamonds.

The dominating figure in the struggle for freedom, the one-time Catholic priest Barthélémy Boganda, was killed in a plane crash in 1959. His nephew, David Dacko, inherited his popularity and became the country's first president on independence the following year. But Dacko did not inherit his uncle's political wisdom. He suppressed opposition and drove the country near to bankruptcy before being ousted by Bokassa in 1965.

Restored in 1979, Dacko was again ousted in 1981. Multiparty elections in 1992 made pro-Western Ange-Félix Patasse president. He survived mutinies by unpaid soldiers, strikes by unpaid civil servants, election-rigging accusations and attempted coups but finally, a 2003 coup brought General Francois Bozize to power.

Careful shoppers *Marketgoers need to think hard before parting with their money.*

Vanishing forest *Timber felling in the south.*

Peanut vendor *Where many are undernourished, peanuts are a good source of protein.*

Cameroon: a mingling of landscapes and peoples

In contrast to most other countries in the region, Cameroon has had only two presidents since independence in 1960. Stability has gone hand in hand with economic success, but the country's human rights record is open to question.

Cameroon is one of the richest countries in sub-Saharan Africa, with a range of exports that allow it to ride the rollercoaster ups and downs of world commodity prices. It produces healthy surpluses of coffee, cocoa, cotton, bananas, rubber and palm oil. And it has claims to oil fields – disputes with Nigeria over the oil of the Bakassi peninsula led to armed clashes in 1994 and 1997.

Some, at least, of its revenues have been invested in health care, transport and education, with the result that Cameroon's adult literacy rate, over 75 per cent, is one of the highest in the continent. On the other hand, corruption is all-pervasive, the government has tried to keep the media under tight control and troops have opened fire on people demonstrating for greater democracy.

Death from the lake

The landscape of Cameroon varies from dense rain forests in the south-west, where Pygmies live by hunter-gathering, to savannah grasslands that reach as far north as the shores of Lake Chad and are roamed by antelopes, giraffes, lions, elephants and hippos. Near the Atlantic coast rises the rain-drenched volcanic peak of

Mont Cameroun – at 13 451 ft (4100 m) the highest mountain in western Africa. Several volcanoes in the Bamileke highlands have crater lakes – one of which, Lake Nyos, discharged a monstrous bubble of carbon dioxide in August 1986. Spilling down the mountainside, the gas, which displaces oxygen from the air, suffocated nearly 2000 people before dispersing. Such dangers apart, the Bamileke highlands are a prosperous region, because of their rich volcanic soil.

Cameroon owes its name to shrimps. The first Portuguese navigators to reach its coast, in 1472, were struck by the abundance of the creatures – *camarão* in Portuguese – in its mangrove-lined bays and inlets. In the centuries that followed, Dutch slave-traders succeeded the Portuguese, and by 1880s the British were intending to

Hail to the chief *A Bamileke chief sits on his bird throne, surrounded by chiefly fetishes.*

Lake in a volcano *Cattle graze on the lip of a crater lake in the Mandara Mountains on the borders of northern Cameroon and Nigeria.*

Mountain village *The pointed roofs of Kirdi houses in the Mandara Mountains.*

Colour-packed market Textiles and food for sale in a Cameroon market.

sponsored a referendum in British Cameroons over their future. The predominantly Muslim north voted to join Nigeria; the Christian and animist south voted to go with the new republic of Cameroon, which then became a federal state.

Authoritarian rule

Ahidjo, continuing as he had started, made Cameroon a one-party state in 1966. He handed over to his prime minister, Paul Biya, a Christian from the south, in 1982. But he regretted this move, for he was almost certainly involved in an attempted coup the next year. Biya suppressed the coup and Ahidjo fled into exile. The Biya regime, too, has shown itself to be heavy handed in dealing with opposition. It has been accused of vote-rigging, and has responded to strikes by setting up military rule in a number of provinces.

bring the region within their empire, but Germany got there before them – by a mere five days – and established a protectorate. During the First World War, the Germans were driven out by a Franco-British force, and after it ended, the territory was divided into French and British mandates.

The French Cameroons, by far the larger territory, won its independence in 1960, after a guerrilla struggle that began in the Bamileke highlands. Ahmadhou Ahidjo, a Muslim from the north, became president and one of his first acts was to turn to the French for help in stamping out a Bamileke rebellion. In 1961, the UN

A taste for tea Limbe – formerly Victoria – was once part of British Cameroons. British influence survives in its tea plantations.

Cameroon's ethnic crossroads

More than 250 different ethnic groups live in Cameroon, reflecting its position on a crossroads of migration routes. Some groups came from the north, in flight from slave-traders or, more recently, from the spread of the Sahara. Bantu-speaking peoples started arriving before 100 BC, pushing the longer-established Babinga Pygmies into the forests of the south-west. Descendants of the early Bantu arrivals include the Bamileke, Bamum and Tikar of the western highlands. Among later Bantu arrivals were the Bassa, Duala, Beti and Fang of the coastal and southern rain-forest zones. In the 18th century, nomadic Fulani herders started moving into the north. They were Muslims and, inspired by the mystic and conqueror Usman dan Fodio, they rebelled against the region's non-Muslim rulers.

One of Usman's commanders, Modibbo Adama, led a jihad, or holy war, in the regions that now bear his name – Adamawa state in Nigeria and the Adamaoua highlands in Cameroon. Adama established a powerful emirate, and those who refused conversion to Islam were driven into the harsher regions of the north, including the Mandara Mountains. Their descendants, mainly animists, are today's Kirdi, from the Fulani word for pagan.

Oil bonanza after Equatorial Guinea's years of tyranny

The discovery of large oil and natural gas fields in the mid 1990s transformed a tiny nation, once among the poorest in Africa, into one of the world's fastest-growing economies.

Equatorial Guinea is a country of two unequal parts: a mainland region, thickly covered with rain forest, and an island part, Bioko, which contains the capital, Malabo. Different as the two parts are, they have borne an equal share of tyranny.

Fever island

The Portuguese navigator Fernão do Pó first sighted Bioko in the early 1470s. In 1778, Portugal signed over the island and mainland territories to Spain, which attempted a settlement on Bioko (then known as Fernando Po), but abandoned it because of the ravages of yellow fever. In the 19th century, bases on the island were leased to the British, who settled some freed slaves there – some Biokans still speak an English-based dialect. Spain established some cocoa and coffee plantations on the mainland in the 1840s, but it was not until 100 years later that it pumped in any serious investment.

Independence came in 1968, and the first president, Francisco Macías Nguema, established a regime that could have rivalled Idi Amin's in Uganda for its human rights abuses. Political opponents and potential rivals were executed or tortured, and churches closed down. It was estimated in the 1970s that one-third of the population was in exile, either voluntary or forced, and that a tenth of

Young capitalists *Children of school age selling goods on the streets of Bata, the chief city of mainland Equatorial Guinea.*

those who remained were in jail. In 1979, Nguema was ousted, put on trial and executed by his nephew, Colonel Teodor Obiang Nguema Mbasogo. The new president began by releasing political prisoners, restoring rights to the Catholic Church and holding multiparty elections. But when he claimed to have won, with 99 per cent support, he was accused of vote-rigging. In June 2002, Obiang announced that an attempted coup had failed: the alleged plotters, including opposition leaders, were jailed for up to 20 years.

The country, meanwhile, has been trumpeted as an economic miracle, thanks to vast reserves of oil and natural gas, discovered off Bioko. Although President Nguema has said that oil revenues are a state secret, estimates rate the country as sub-Saharan Africa's 3rd largest oil producer, and the world's fastest growing economy. Opponents of the regime claim, however, that the bulk of the benefits of these riches go to the president's supporters among the Fang people.

Cocoa workers on Bioko *The woman in the middle splits open the pods to remove the beans, which she throws onto the pile on her left.*

São Tomé and Príncipe: from slavery to democracy

The tiny state of São Tomé and Príncipe consists of two volcanic islands and a few islets in the Gulf of Guinea. Blessed with fertile soils and high rainfall, it was once the world's biggest producer of sugar. Later, it was the biggest cocoa producer. Today, the country hopes that offshore oil may pull it out of poverty.

Just 136 000 people make up the population of São Tomé and Príncipe. Yet that small number includes five distinct groups: the *forros*, who are the descendants of African slaves, freed in 1875; the *mestiços*, mixed-race descendants of European settlers and African slaves; the *angolares*, descended from a shipload of Angolan slaves bound for Brazil who were wrecked off São Tomé in 1540; the *serviçais*, contract labourers from nearby African countries, and the *tongas*, who are the island-born children of *serviçais*. The islands were uninhabited when first sighted by Portuguese navigators in 1471.

Huge foreign debt

São Tomé and Príncipe are fertile, mountainous and for eight months of the year wet. Annual rainfall of 39 in (1000 mm) in the coastal areas rises to 200 in (5100 mm) in the mountainous interior. Cocoa, grown in large plantations (or *rocas*) in the coastal low-

Grand entrance *São Tomé's hospital, beautifully preserved from the Portuguese colonial era.*

lands, is by far the biggest export. Tuna fishing is important among communities of *angolares* in the south of São Tomé. Vulnerable to the fluctuations of world cocoa prices and burdened with a huge foreign debt, the country is heavily dependent on foreign aid, which in 2000 added up to more than US$236 per person.

The Portuguese established sugar plantations, importing slaves from Africa to work them, and briefly in the early 16th century, São Tomé was the world's largest sugar producer. In 1530, a blind slave, Yon Gato, led the first of several rebellions. Runaway slaves found refuge in the mountains of the interior, from where they raided the plantations. In 1574, their most famous leader, the *angolare* Amador, set fire to the capital.

Slavery and the abuse of labour have been a running theme in the islands' history. They were a staging post in the slave trade between Africa and Brazil. After Portugal abolished

slavery, the islands' landowners imported indentured labourers from Africa, working them in conditions that were virtually identical to slavery. By the 1890s cocoa had been introduced as a plantation crop, and for several years in the early 20th century São Tomé and Príncipe was the world's largest producer. But the conditions of the labourers led many European manufacturers to boycott its produce. As late as 1953 Portuguese troops opened fire on *forro* labourers who refused to work on plantations at Batepá on São Tomé, killing 1000.

Outrage at the massacre helped to fuel a left-wing nationalist movement. Independence came in 1975, and from the start the republic was a left-wing, one-party state. Plantations were nationalised and ties established with the communist bloc. During the 1980s, however, President Manuel Pinto da Costa, realising the need for Western aid, allowed multiparty elections. The austerity measures of his successor, Miguel Trovoada, provoked unrest, and in 2001 he was succeeded by a businessman, Fradique de Menezes, who promised to modernise the economy using revenue from licenses to exploit the offshore oil fields due to be auctioned in 2004.

Paradise awaiting discovery *Palm trees, hibiscus flowers and an offshore islet compose a perfect tropical scene. The islands' remoteness makes it difficult for them to exploit their tourist potential.*

Oil and prosperous times in Gabon

Thanks to its oil revenues, Gabon is one of the most prosperous countries in Africa. Other mineral riches include some of the largest-known reserves of manganese, as well as iron ore and uranium. The country's authoritarian and pro-Western leader, President Omar Bongo, has held power since 1967.

Bringing the country together   *European capital helped to finance the Transgabonais railway, completed in 1986, linking Libreville with the interior.*

A hooded cape worn by Portuguese seamen gave Gabon its name. The shape of the estuary where the capital Libreville now stands reminded early Portuguese navigators of the hoods of their *gabão* cloaks. The name of the estuary was eventually transferred to the whole territory.

Modern Gabon is thinly populated even by African standards. A little larger in area than the United Kingdom, it has a population of around 1.3 million people, drawn from 40 Bantu-speaking ethnic groups. It is also one of the most urbanised countries in Africa – more than 80 per cent of Gabonese live in Libreville and the other towns and cities of the coastal region. They enjoy one of the continent's highest standards of living, with an average annual income of US$3698, compared with $661 in neighbouring Congo (Brazzaville). Rain forest – whose tropical hardwoods were Gabon's chief source of wealth before the discovery of offshore oil and natural gas – covers more than three-quarters of the country.

Slaves for guns

From the 15th century on, a series of coastal kingdoms grew powerful from commerce with Portuguese, Dutch, English and French traders, exchanging slaves, ivory, beeswax, ebony and animal skins for European iron tools, textiles, alcohol and later firearms. In the end, the French established themselves as Gabon's colonial masters in the late 1830s and early 1840s.

At independence in 1960, the new republic's first leader was Léon M'ba. Once exiled by the French authorities as a revolutionary troublemaker, he now angered many of his countrymen by his conservative, pro-French policies. His choice of loyalties paid off, however. When the military ousted

Ethnic diversity   *The Fang people are the largest ethnic group, amounting to about a third of the population.*

him in a coup in 1964, it was French troops who reinstated him. After his death in 1967, his chosen successor, Albert-Bernard Bongo (who later converted to Islam and added Omar to his name) turned Gabon into a one-party state and spent US$120 million building a presidential palace.

For many years political opposition was neutered by oil prosperity, but in the late 1980s a drop in world oil prices helped to trigger another round of discontent. After demonstrations in Libreville, Bongo changed the constitution to allow multiparty elections.

Log jam   *Timber from the rain forests is floated down the river arteries, including the Ogooué, Komo and Mbeï, to ports on the coast.*

After being accused of rigging the election of 1993, he claimed a winning vote of 99.97 per cent in 1998.

Gabon has some of the best health care in Africa, financed by its oil riches. It also had the shining example of the Alsatian-born theologian, doctor and Nobel peace prize winner, Albert Schweitzer, who arrived in Gabon just before the First World War and died there in 1965. The hospital he built at Lambaréné on the Ogooué river is still functioning.

Congo: unhappy past, uncertain future

African kingdoms in what is now Congo (Brazzaville) grew rich from the slave trade. In the colonial era, private companies made big profits by exploiting the land and the people. Today, the country is ravaged by conflict.

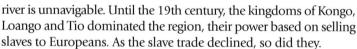

Congo is a rich land, paralysed by internal conflicts. It is one of Africa's largest oil producers, and also exports sugar, coffee, cocoa and diamonds. But it has been plagued by civil war since the early 1990s, and its history is stained by a century of colonial exploitation. Rain forest covers 65 per cent of the country. About one-third of the people subsist on the land. The capital, Brazzaville, stands inland beside the Congo's Malebo Pool, below which the river is unnavigable. Until the 19th century, the kingdoms of Kongo, Loango and Tio dominated the region, their power based on selling slaves to Europeans. As the slave trade declined, so did they.

From river to sea *The 364 mile (586 km) Congo-Océan railway links the water highways of the Congo basin with the Atlantic.*

A delicate balance *Bringing in firewood from the forest.*

Railway of death

In the 1880s, the Italian-born French explorer Pierre Savorgnan de Brazza, after whom the capital is named, persuaded local rulers to put themselves under French protection. France divided it into 'concessions' which were farmed out to private companies to exploit as they saw fit. The resultant cruelties caused such an outrage in France that de Brazza was sent back to investigate. He died on the journey, and the abuses continued. Worst of all was the building of the Congo-Océan railway, connecting Brazzaville with the coast. It cost an estimated 17 000 lives.

Against such a background, it is not surprising that, following independence in 1960, the country should be prey to instability. In 1963, Congo became the first former French colony to turn to Marxism. Denis Sassou-Nguesso, a former paratroop colonel, who came to power in 1979, was initially pro-Soviet. But he looked to the West for investment, and in 1990, following the collapse of the Soviet empire, he formally renounced Marxism. Losing the 1992 presidential election, he handed over to Patrick Lissouba.

But in 1993 he challenged the results of the parliamentary elections, again won by Lissouba.

Protests led to violence and by the end of the year 2000 people had died. Sassou-Nguesso's power base lay in the north, while Lissouba's support was mainly in the south. By 1997 Sassou-Nguesso had captured Brazzaville, forcing Lissouba to flee. A peace accord was signed in 1999, and elections were held in March 2002. Sassou-Nguesso won but his chief rivals, Lissouba and Bernard Kolelas, had not been allowed to stand. In June 2002, around 100 people were killed in the capital during fighting between the army and supporters of Kolelas

Tourist potential *Long sandy beaches line the coast near Pointe-Noire.*

War and misery in the Democratic Republic of Congo

Mineral riches have proved a curse for the Democratic Republic of Congo (formerly Zaire). Rather than enriching the people, they have been plundered by both outsiders and the country's own rulers.

During a 'reign' of nearly 32 years, President Mobutu built 11 palaces and amassed a fortune estimated at US$6 billion. Mobutu, a general when he seized power in 1965, received generous American backing during the Cold War, for he was staunchly anti-Soviet. He was also an enthusiastic Africaniser, pursuing a policy he called 'Authenticity'. He changed the country's name to Zaire (from a local word meaning 'Big River'), dropped his forenames, Joseph Désiré, and renamed himself Mobutu Sese Seko (Mobutu the all-powerful).

Western styles *An animated discussion in 'Kin', a popular abbreviation for the capital, Kinshasa.*

Congo, known by its present name since Mobutu's overthrow in 1997, is 9½ times the size of the United Kindgom, with a population of 51 million. It has some of the world's biggest reserves of copper, cobalt and industrial diamonds, as well as zinc, cadmium, gold, silver and some offshore oil. Elephants live in the rain forests that cover 60 per cent of the country, but poachers take a yearly toll reaching into thousands.

The shaming of King Leopold

In 1874, King Leopold II of Belgium sponsored the explorer Henry Morton Stanley on a voyage down the Congo river, thereby staking his claim to treat the entire vast region as his personal property, to be farmed out to private companies. A scandal over the treatment of slave labour on rubber plantations led the Belgian government to take control in 1908. After independence, in 1960, the country fell into anarchy. The army mutinied. The prime minister, Patrice Lumumba, was murdered, almost certainly with CIA backing. The copper-rich region of Katanga broke away under Moise Tshombe, and it took UN troops to end the rebellion. Mobutu, in 1965, seemed to offer stability. Instead, corruption and mismanagement plunged the country into debt.

By the mid 1990s a rebellion was under way in the east, partly caused by violence spilling over from the civil war in Rwanda.

Mobutu fled before the rebels took the capital, Kinshasa, in May 1997. More misery was to come. The new president, rebel leader Laurent-Désiré Kabila, faced another rebellion in the east, backed by Rwanda and Uganda. The conflict widened as he turned for help to Angola, Namibia and Zimbabwe. In January 2001, Kabila was assassinated by one of his bodyguards. His son Joseph took over. Despite UN intervention, the fighting continued. At stake was the chance to loot copper, gold and diamonds. By May 2001, an estimated 2.5 million people had lost their lives in three years of war.

Earth's riches *A copper mine near Kolwezi.*

A tendency to split

Congo breaks into three large economic zones, with poor communications between them and a natural tendency to go their own ways. In the south, the region of Katanga (also known as Shaba), which tried to break away in the 1960s, holds most of the mineral wealth.

The north and north-east depend on agriculture. In the west, Kinshasa is the centre, in peaceful times at least, of political and administrative power and the service industries.

Following Jesus *Pygmies in the Ituri forest region of the east take part in an Easter procession.*

Angola's thirty years' war

In both duration and destructiveness the civil war that has raged in Angola since independence could almost vie with the Thirty Years' War that ravaged Germany in the 17th century. This vast land, potentially one of the richest in Africa, now faces starvation.

When the Portuguese arrived on the Angolan coast at the end of the 15th century, they made such a good first impression that they converted the local Bakongo king, Nzinga Nkuwu, to Roman Catholicism. Relations soured, however, in the years that followed, as the newcomers took more and more slaves from the region. The Portuguese founded Luanda, now the capital, in 1575 but did not move into the highlands of the interior until the 19th century, and did not subdue them until 1920.

Filling the power vacuum

Angola's independence came in 1975, after a fierce guerrilla struggle, but the vacuum left by the departing Portuguese led to a collapse of the economy, and opened the way to a power struggle that reflected the divide between the coastal region and the interior. Two organisations dominated the nationalist movement. The Marxist MPLA (Popular Movement for the Liberation of Angola) had its power base among the Mbundu people of the coast. Jonas Savimbi's UNITA (National Union for the Total Independence of Angola) had its strongholds among the Ovimbundu of the interior plateaus. In the decades of fighting that followed, diamonds from the interior helped to finance UNITA, while the MPLA had the revenues from Angola's offshore oil and natural gas fields.

By the end of 1976, the MPLA was established as the government in Luanda, while UNITA was fighting a guerrilla rebellion. Both had outside help. Alarmed at the prospect of a Marxist Angola – a land rich not only in diamonds and oil, but also in iron ore, manganese, copper and phosphates – South Africa and the USA supported UNITA. The government received arms from the Soviet Union and 30 000 troops from Cuba. In 1979, a Soviet-trained engineer, José Eduardo dos Santos, became MPLA's leader.

Taking aim   A UNITA guerrilla fighter. Revenues from diamonds illegally exported from UNITA-held territory helped to keep the civil war going.

Hundreds of thousands died in the fighting, many of them victims of land mines. Entire villages were deserted by their terror-stricken inhabitants, and in many parts of the country farming virtually came to a standstill. A series of attempted ceasefires came to nothing, but in the new world that emerged after the end of the Cold War and of apartheid, UNITA lost most of its international support. And after Savimbi was killed by government forces, in February 2002, hopes grew for an enduring peace. The problem facing Angola as thousands of refugees streamed back to their ravaged home towns and villages was not war but its aftermath – starvation.

A safe home   Despite the civil war, and its constant drain on government funds, some development projects have been put in hand, including housing for refugees (right).

The Cabinda enclave

Cabinda is a pocket of Angolan territory separated from the rest of the country by the mouth of the Congo river, belonging to the Democratic Republic of Congo. Although small, it is vital to the national economy because more than half Angola's offshore oil production comes from rigs off Cabinda's 56 mile (90 km) coastline. It also has phosphates, diamonds and manganese, as well as coffee and cocoa plantations. A Front for the Liberation of the Cabinda Enclave (FLEC) has been active since the mid 1970s.

Harbour view   Luanda's seafront corniche road, inherited from the Portuguese, is one of the most beautiful in Africa.

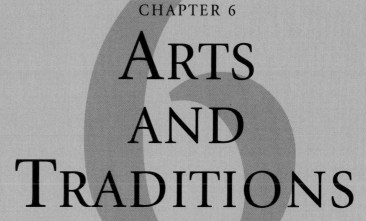

CHAPTER 6

ARTS AND TRADITIONS

Africa's artistic heritage has not only survived in the modern age – it has thrived. Whatever the continent's economic and political ills, its traditional arts and crafts – from making masks to ritual dancing, storytelling to wood-carving, music-making to fabric design – have displayed astonishing vitality. They have also spread their influence well beyond their native continent. In painting, African masks inspired Picasso and contributed to the Cubist movement. In music, an unexpected result of slavery was the birth in the Americas of jazz and a number of other musical styles, from the rumba to the blues. Africa's gift to the New World was handsomely paid back when gramophone records, radio, cinema and later television brought the music back home. Cross-fertilisation, on its return journey, created a gallery of new sounds, such as Afro-beat and highlife, not just for Africa, but for the world.

A Senegalese griot – a traditional storyteller, oral historian and minstrel.

Living to the beat of music

African musicians, from Cesaria Evora to Youssou n'Dour, are winning audiences outside their own countries. They tap into their own musical traditions and fuse them with Latin and North American styles – themselves often indebted to the songs that were sung on plantations worked by African slaves.

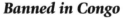

Just as in the West, the 1960s in Africa were a good time for popular music. In the towns and cities of newly independent countries, new bands were mixing traditional musical styles and beats with the different, yet sometimes strangely familiar, sounds that came from across the Atlantic. In the western Congo, Kinshasa was particularly vibrant. Here, the Afro-Cuban rumba had already in the first half of the 20th century been 're-Africanised' as the Congolese rumba. Now, in the hands of musicians such as Tabu Ley Rochereau, a new version was emerging, known as 'soukous' – from the French *secousse*, 'shake' – characterised by rich melodies, fast drumming and boisterous lyrics in the region's lingua franca, Lingala. Tabu Ley was to become known as the 'African Sinatra', and to make an international name for himself.

In Guinea and Mali, the style known as 'Manding swing' was born, in which the musical traditions of the Malinke (also known as Mandingo) people were blended with Latin influences and played on the electric guitar and keyboard. In Ghana and Nigeria, 'highlife' – a reference to the supposed lifestyle of

Cesaria Evora, the barefoot diva

In the Cape Verde islands, a mingling of African and Portuguese traditions produced the songs of nostalgia, sadness and deprivation known as *morna*. The unquestioned queen of *morna*, Cesaria Evora, won international fame in the 1990s, after years of singing in down-at-heel bars. Her impassioned presence and husky voice have earned her comparison with Edith Piaf. Because she always performs in bare feet, she is also known as the 'barefoot diva'.

the people who danced it – mingled local rhythms with a Westernised big band sound. By the 1970s, Ali Farka Toure, a self-taught musician from Mali, had discovered the music of African-American blues singers such as Ray Charles and Otis Redding, and was fashioning a weave of blues with the Arabic-influenced traditions of his home region around Timbuktu.

Banned in Congo

By the mid 1990s, a young singer in Kinshasa, Koffi Olomidé, with his band Quartier Latin, was giving soukous a new twist, with a harder-edged, often sexually suggestive sound. Olomidé called this style 'ndombolo' – from the Lingala word for 'buttocks'. His album *La Loi*, released in 1997, was banned in Congo-Kinshasa, because some of its lyrics were taken to be critical of the newly installed Kabila regime. By then, the Senegalese Youssou n'Dour, with his band The Super Etoile, was an established international star in the local style known as 'mbalax', which incorporates reggae influences. He was quoted admiringly by American singers such as Paul Simon.

Another rising mbalax star, Cheikh Lô, was a member of a strict Muslim sect, the Baye Fall, notable for wearing dreadlocks and patchwork clothing. Reggae may have begun in the West Indies, but dreadlocks did not. Long before the West Indian

African xylophone A balafon player in Burkina. The calabashes beneath the keys create a rich, resonating sound.

Rastafarian movement began, they were worn by members of the Baye Fall, founded in 19th-century Senegal as an inner circle within the Mouride brotherhood. Dedicated to poverty and hard work, they sang songs known as *zikr*, to honour Allah.

A lute-like harp and a xylophone

The instruments used by these performers have been a mix of Western and traditional African. A typical soukous band might include guitars, bass, drums, brass and singers – as many as 20 members in all. Most African drums are made from either hollowed-out logs or calabashes. Traditionally, they were used for sending messages as well as for making music. Stringed instruments include the West African *kora*, a large calabash with an animal skin stretched over it and a wooden neck, usually with around 20 strings. Although it looks like a lute, it is played more like a harp. The *balafon*, also from West Africa, is a kind of xylophone, in which small wooden slats are tied together, with calabash sounding boxes beneath.

Talking drums   A school for young drummers (left) in Dakar, the Senegalese capital.

Superstar from Senegal   Youssou n'Dour, the acknowledged king of mbalax, a fusion of African and Caribbean rhythms that has won fans around the world.

All in the family   A street musician playing the balaton in Guinea. Children develop a love of the instrument in their earliest years.

131

From tradition to haute couture

The clothes Africans wear are known for their bright colours and bold designs. Clothing in Africa has a multitude of meanings. The quality of the material indicates rank and status, while designs are put to many uses, including advertising and political propaganda.

Benin fashion *A dressmaker's shop in Cotonou.*

Good posture comes early to African women, for when a young girl needs to carry a heavy load, she learns to balance it on her head. This natural elegance is often evident, too, in the traditional costumes of the continent. The wrap-round skirt known as a *pagne*, a *sorsa* or a *zaara*, is near-universal wear for women in Central and West Africa. It consists simply of a length of cloth, wrapped round the waist and tucked in on the left-hand side.

Completing the outfit are a tight-fitting blouse and another *pagne*, folded in half and knotted in the small of the back – in many places, this second *pagne* is for married women only. The cloth for *pagnes* is usually lightweight cotton, bought in lengths of 2 yards, 6 yards or 12 yards – yards are the units of cloth measurement even in French-speaking countries.

The designs on the fabric are a language of their own. At their simplest, they are geometric patterns. But often they carry messages. One common design, called 'Your Feet, My Feet', shows two pairs of footprints, one against a yellow background, the other on red. The message is that if the husband strays after other women, his wife will be close behind him. Another design, 'Nails of Madame Thérèse', featured the fingernails of Madame Thérèse Houphouët-Boigny, wife of the late president of Ivory Coast. A design could be taken from advertising – the logo of, say, the national electricity company. It could be part of a publicity campaign to raise awareness of a disease such as AIDS. Or, during an election campaign, it could carry the face of a politician. In some parts of Africa, both men and women wear the kaftan-like *boubou* – a wide-sleeved tunic, held in place by a sash.

Dazzling kente *cloth*

There is a wide range of traditional hand-woven textiles for special occasions. The Kuba people of Congo-Kinshasa weave a surprisingly soft fabric from fibres of the raffia palm. In Mali, the Sahel region is famed for its 'mud cloth', or *bogolan*, in which mud from different sources is used to give the cloth hues of red, yellow, orange, brown, even white. Even better

Looks traditional, but ... *A cloth seller in Lomé, Togo (above). The cheapest fabrics are imported from Europe, with their designs printed on them.*

Badge of a wife *In many regions, women wear a second* pagne *skirt to show that they are married.*

Pioneer of African fashion

Seidnaly Sidhamed Alphadi was one of the first African designers to establish a worldwide reputation. He was born in Timbuktu, Mali, in 1957, but grew up in Niger, where his father was a businessman. He went to Paris to study tourism, returning to Niger as director of tourism. But in 1983 he decided to devote himself full time to his first love – fashion. His first collection, shown in Paris two years later, was an overnight success. Drawing inspiration from the Songhai, Bororo, Hausa and Zarma costumes of his homeland, he has presented shows in many of the world's major fashion centres, from New York to Tokyo. In 1998 he fulfilled a long-held ambition when he founded the International Festival of African Fashion (FIMA), to take place every other year as a showcase for African designers.

Couturier and models   *Paris-based Alphadi during a photographic shoot in the savannah near Niamey.*

known is the *kente* cloth of the Ashanti people of Ghana. Strips of cloth, around 4 in (10 cm) wide, and each with a different design in gold, yellow, red, black, green or blue, are sewn together into dazzlingly multicoloured lengths about 12 ft by 8 ft (3.7 m by 2.4 m). Traditionally, only men and women of a certain rank in Ashanti society are allowed to wear *kente*. Men drape it, toga-like, around them, leaving the right shoulder bare. Women wrap it around the body, often with a matching blouse.

Today Niger, tomorrow Paris

Not surprisingly, this rich heritage of textiles and costumes has inspired talented young fashion designers to seek a wider stage. A number have moved to Europe – usually to Paris – and, like Alphadi from Niger, have set up their own fashion houses. Mali's Chris Seydou, who died in 1994, incorporated Malian 'mud cloth' into his designs. In London, the Ghanaian Oswald Boateng, with premises just off Savile Row, established himself in the mid 1990s as one of Britain's most highly regarded tailors.

Pathé'O – full name Ainé Pathé Ouédraogo – was born in Burkina, but lives and works in Abidjan, Ivory Coast. He is famous as the man who makes the richly coloured trademark shirts of the former South African president, Nelson Mandela. Kofi Ansah, trained in Britain but now working in his native Ghana, uses *kente* cloth, as well as traditional batik and tie-dye techniques, to make Western-style clothes. The Senegalese Oumou Sy has long been a leading figure in the West African fashion world. Also based in Senegal, the young designer Claire Kane has called her label '100%

Dripping with gold   *The Ivorian jewellery designer, Mickael Kra, at an international festival.*

Dakar'. She uses only local materials hand-woven, using traditional methods, by local weavers.

The blossoming of African fashion has met some opposition from extremist Muslims. In November 2000, the second International Festival of African Fashion, organised by the Paris-based Alphadi in his native Niger, triggered demonstrations in the capital Niamey. Clerics protested that the festival was 'satanic', would encourage debauchery, help to spread AIDS and 'call down the wrath of Allah on our people'. An enraged crowd, 800 strong, gathered outside the parliament building, and was dispersed only when police used tear gas and batons.

Beauty and function in Africa's arts and crafts

Africa's heritage of craftsmanship began among isolated communities, using the materials to hand. Nomadic herders such as the Tuareg and Fulani developed great skill at leatherworking. The forest-living Ashanti carved stools that became emblems of kingship. Masks are near-universal and include many different styles: they are worn for special rites such as those marking the phases of the agricultural year. Even the face and body can become a canvas for artistic expression, through the practice of making incisions to leave scars that are a mark of status.

Taking shape *Fang statuette from Gabon.*

According to an African legend, the first mask was made by a mother to punish a naughty child who had ignored her warnings and strayed too close to the edge of a well. She took a calabash, painted a frightening face on it and used it to scare the child into better behaviour. Masks that can be terrifying in their aspect are found throughout Central and West Africa. The Fang people of Cameroon, Equatorial Guinea and Gabon, for instance, make striking-looking masks, with a face outlined in black on a white background, which they use in rituals to punish sorcerers.

In the early 20th century, the beauty and simplicity of African masks came as a revelation to Picasso and other European artists, helping to inspire the Cubist movement. But to an African, a mask is never simply an artistic object. It is a key element to be used in ceremonies during the farming year or at the turning points of life.

The antelope men

When the Bobo people of Burkina, for example, plant their crops, they wear wooden masks as they dance to invoke the favour of their rain god, Do. The masks have geometric patterns painted on them in black, white and red, and are shaped to represent different creatures – owls, scorpions, antelopes and butterflies. The fearsome 'Bundu' masks of the Mende people of Sierra Leone, covering the

The matmaker *A Dogon craftsman in Mali.*

Millet scoop
From Côte d'Ivoire.

134

entire body, are worn during initiation rites. Often, particular rituals are the responsibility of special societies. One such brotherhood, among the Bambara of Mali, is devoted to Tyiwara, the spirit who taught humans how to farm, and usually represented as an antelope. Twice a year, when crops are planted and harvested, members of the society, wearing antelope headdresses, perform a dance involving spectacular antelope-like leaps in the air.

Meal with a message

The peoples of Central Africa are renowned for their sculptures and carvings, especially of figures depicting the ancestors of chiefs, shown kneeling, sitting or standing with serene expressions on their faces. Among the Woyo people of the region around the mouth of the Congo, the skills of the carvers are also put to more domestic use. Traditionally, when a young woman gets married, she is given a set of carved wooden pot lids, each depicting a different proverb about married life. If a wife is unhappy with her husband for whatever reason, she covers the pot or dish with an appropriate lid when she serves him his meal. He is then obliged to discuss the issue with her, in front of witnesses.

Among nomadic peoples, such as the Fulani of Mali, Senegal, Nigeria and other lands, prized possessions need to be portable, and the skills of the leatherworker are admired. For the Yoruba of

Traditional pottery Earthenware storage jars, in Guinea.

Nigeria, who cut scars in their faces to show which lineage they belong to, the 'scarifier' is a respected figure.

Contact with the West has inevitably had an impact on African arts and crafts. As early as the 16th century, craftspeople in the coastal regions of Sierra Leone were producing ivory carvings, based on traditional styles, but aimed at the Portuguese market. In more recent times tourism, while in many ways reducing the impact and authenticity of African arts and crafts, may also have saved some of them. Traditional items of everyday ware, such as the earthenware pitchers used to store millet beer in parts of Mali, have great aesthetic value. But in the daily battle for survival, they often lose out to modern mass-produced goods, which are cheaper and more durable. To preserve the old styles, governments have happily encouraged production for the tourist trade. The ancestor figures of the Mangbetu people of northern Congo (Dem. Rep.) were once made only for chiefs; now, their sculptors carve similar figures for sale to visitors.

Patterns of tourism have also had their effect. Until the 1960s, Westerners visiting or working in Africa probably came by ship. For them, it was feasible to take home a chair from Benin, carved out of a single piece of wood. In the age of air travel, tourists look for items that are light and easy to pack.

Handing on Old people, such as this basket-maker, pass on skills to the next generation.

Earth furnace Bronze casting is an ancient craft in Nigeria.

Africa's modern artists

The purpose of traditional African art was to meet the needs of the community, rather than to express the artist's urge to create. Carvings, for example, were used in ancestor worship or to ensure the favour of the gods. Modern African artists draw on Western traditions, as well as their own. The combination can be powerful.

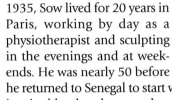

Through a glass *The Senegalese Babacar Lo is known for his paintings on the back of glass.*

Rows of numbered terracotta faces stand for the anonymous victims of the 1994 genocide in Rwanda, when mobs of Hutu massacred thousands of Tutsi, their former overlords. Nearby, a group of sculptures called 'The All-Seeing Eye' shows an eye on a television-shaped oblong. 'The world looked on …' comments their creator, Kofi Setordji, 'as hundreds of bodies floated down the Kagera river, and nothing was done.' A huge figure holding out a pair of scales represents the call for justice.

Vanishing cultures

Born in Accra in 1957, Setordji was already well known in Ghana when he conceived his memorial to the estimated 800,000 victims of the Rwandan genocide – the figure includes those who died from starvation or disease. The memorial uses a variety of materials – wood, metal, clay, waste material and paint. For his older contemporary, Ousmane Sow, the disappearing cultures of Africa have been an important inspiration. Born in the

Vibrant hues *Scenes from the markets are a typical theme of the Poto-Poto artists.*

Senegalese capital Dakar in 1935, Sow lived for 20 years in Paris, working by day as a physiotherapist and sculpting in the evenings and at weekends. He was nearly 50 before he returned to Senegal to start working full-time at his art. In 1984, inspired by the photographs of the German Leni Riefenstahl, he began his first major series of sculptures, depicting Nuba wrestlers from Sudan. Later in the 1980s and 1990s, he did a series dedicated to the Masai, the Zulu and Fulani herders, each time trying to capture the 'soul' of the people he was commemorating.

Secret formula

He also found a parallel between the effects of colonialism on Africa and the conquest of the American West. One of his best-known works is a series dedicated to the Battle of Little Big Horn, the last major victory of American Indians over the whites.

His works have a steel framework, covered with coarse cloth, and one of their intriguing aspects is the chocolate-coloured substance he uses to treat them. It has 20 or so ingredients, including glue, which he leaves to brew in his garden for years at a time. The exact formula is a secret he keeps to himself.

Finishing touches *Ousmane Sow at work on 'The Free Man', an image of the African-American returning to Africa.*

The Poto-Poto Art School

French artist Pierre Lods established one of Africa's most influential art schools in the Poto-Poto district of Brazzaville in 1951. To encourage truly African painting, Lods banned any reproductions of Western art. The resulting paintings depicted local scenes and motifs in blocks of brilliant colour – a style that spread rapidly across the continent.

The examining eye: writing and movie-making in Africa

The stories told by modern African writers are the story of Africa itself: of the high hopes that came with independence, but all too often foundered in a sea of corruption; of the resilience, despite all setbacks, of the African people.

The Nigerian novelist Chinua Achebe published his first novel, *Things Fall Apart*, in 1958. It was a study of the impact of colonialism and Christianity on a traditional African village. By the time his later novel, *Man of the People*, was published in 1966, Nigeria had been independent for six years, and he had turned his eye to a new theme: corruption and disappointed idealism.

Contemporary African writing owes much to the *négritude* movement, which emerged in the 1930s among French-speaking black intellectuals, including the poet, and Senegal's future first president, Léopold Sédar Senghor. For them, the task of black writers was to reassert African values in the face of dominant Western culture. By the 1960s, however, the hopes of independence were being betrayed by corruption and repression, and a new generation of writers was turning a more critical eye on its own societies.

The price of speaking out

In French-speaking Senegal, the Muslim writer Sheikh Hamidou Kane published his autobiographical novel *Ambiguous Adventure* in 1961, about a young man torn between the values of his ancestors and those of Western materialism. In Ghana, Ayi Kwei Armah's *The Beautyful Ones Are Not Yet Born* (1968) is about an honest man whose honesty brings him only contempt. In Nigeria, the playwright, poet and novelist Wole Soyinka drew on both the dramatic traditions of his own Yoruba people and Western experimental modernism. He paid a personal price for political outspokenness: he spent two years in prison, much of it in solitary confinement, during the Biafran war. Later, however, he achieved international recognition, becoming the first African to win the Nobel prize for literature, in 1986. Another Nigerian writer, Ken Saro-Wiwa, was executed by order of General Sani Abacha, for leading a protest against his regime.

By the 1990s, African writers were becoming known internationally. In 1991 the novelist Ben Okri, from the Urhobo people of southern Nigeria, won Britain's Booker prize with *The Famished Road*. In 2000, after a writing career spanning five decades, Ahmadou Kourouma, from the Malinke people of Ivory Coast, won the French Prix Renaudot with his novel *Allah Is Not Obliged*, about a child soldier fighting in the civil war in Liberia.

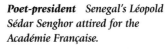

Poet-president Senegal's Léopold Sédar Senghor attired for the Académie Française.

A way with words Ahmadou Kourouma of Ivory Coast, winner of France's prestigious Prix Renaudot.

On location The Malian Souleymane Cissé (below) has established himself as one of Africa's most successful directors.

African cinema

Africa has long been used as an exotic backdrop by film-makers, but it was not until the 1960s that a truly home-grown cinema emerged. The films made in the early years of independence often looked back on the evils of colonialism. Then, in 1966, the Senegalese Ousmane Sembène caused a sensation at an arts festival in Dakar with his first feature-length movie, *La Noire de …* The infant industry gained added impetus through the founding, in 1972, of Fespaco, a biennial festival held in Ouagadougou, the capital of Burkina. By the 1980s, African cinema was reaching world audiences with such films as *Yeelen* (1989) from the Malian director Souleymane Cissé.

MAPS, FACTS AND FIGURES

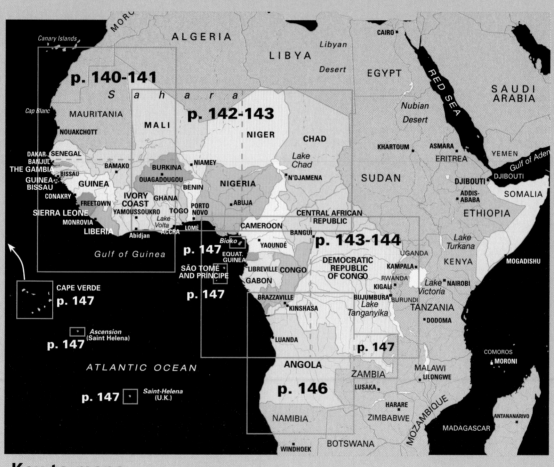

Key to maps

Place names

■ CAPITAL   ● City

● Major city   • Town

Borders

——————— International land frontier

- - - - - - - - International maritime frontier

Topography

▲ Mt Cameroon
4100 m   Summit

**MONTS
MUGITA**   Mountain range

Key to elevation tints

Metres

4000
3000
2000
1000
500
200
0

Key to depth tints

Metres

- 200
- 1000
- 2000

F

Bou Bernous

Erg Chech

Hamada du Draa

Hamada Tounassine

MALI

Bamba

Bourem

Gourma-Rharous

Niger

Timbuktu
(Tombouctou)

Hombori

Tanezrouft

Azaouad

Taoudenni

Douentza

Tanezrouft

Diré

Lac
Débo

Ngouma

Korientzé

Niafounké

Araouane

E

Chegga

Ras el Mâ

Goundam

Lac
Faguibine

JEBEL OUARKZIZ

Tindouf

Gara Djebilet

El Hank

Ouâlata

Néma

**Hodh
Ech
Chargui**

Bassikounou

Sokolo

MOROCCO

Ain Ben Tili

Z e m m o u r

S A H A R A

Nara

D

O. Draa

Tan Tan

Bir Moghrein

Tichit

Ayoun el Atrous

Timbedgha

Ballé

Baoulé

Tan Tan Beach

Semara

Oued Saguia al-Hamra

Galtat Zemmour

M e k t e i r

**Hodh
El Gharbi**

Nioro

Tamchekket

C

FUERTEVENTURA

Cap Juby

Tarfaya

Boukra

Zouérat

Kediet ej Jill
915 m

Fdérik

A d r a r

Guelb er-Richât

Ouadâne

Chinguetti

Tidjikja

Tagant

Aoukâr

Kiffa

Kayes

Bakel

Sélibabi

GRAN CANARIA

Cap Boujdour

Boujdour

El Aaiun (Laayoune)

**WESTERN
SAHARA**

Choum

Atar

Oujeft

Akjoujt

Maudjéria

Nigër-Ko

Gorgol

Kaédi

Matam

SENEGAL

Tambacounda

B

HIERRO

Dakhla

Techlé

T i r i s

Azeffal

Khatt Atoui

Âguerguer

NOUAKCHOTT

Boutilimit

Aleg

Bogué

Boghé

Kanel

Sénégal

Podor

Dagana

Linguère

Touba

Mbacké

Diourbel

Mbar

Saloum

Kaffrine

Kuntaur

Cap Barbas

Noûâmghar

Râs Timirist

P. N. DU
DJOUDJ

Lac de
Guier

St Louis

Louga

Mékhé

Thiès

**ATLANTIC
OCEAN**

La Gouéra
Cap Blanc

PARC NATIONAL DU
BANC D'ARGUIN

Nouadhibou

MAURITANIA

Pointe des
Almadies

DAKAR

Cap Vert

Rufisque

I. DE
GORÉE

Mbour

Joal-Fadiout

Kaolack

Bakau

BANJUL

Serekunda

Gambia

Tropic of Cancer

140

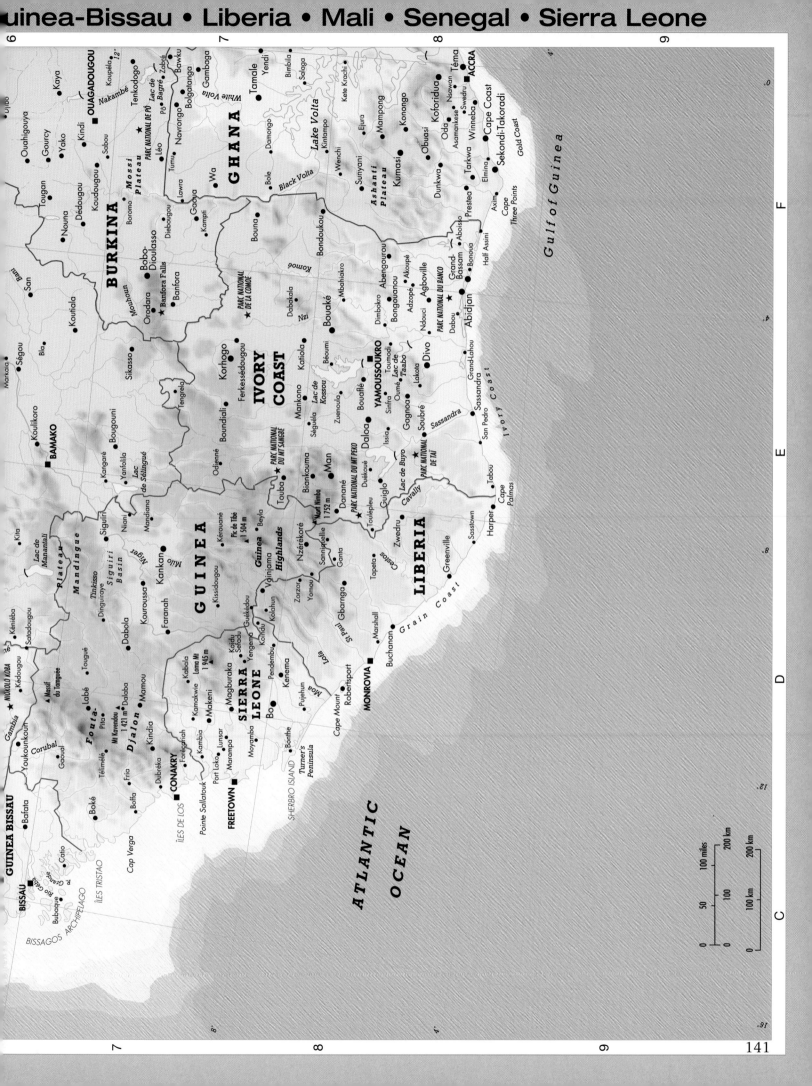

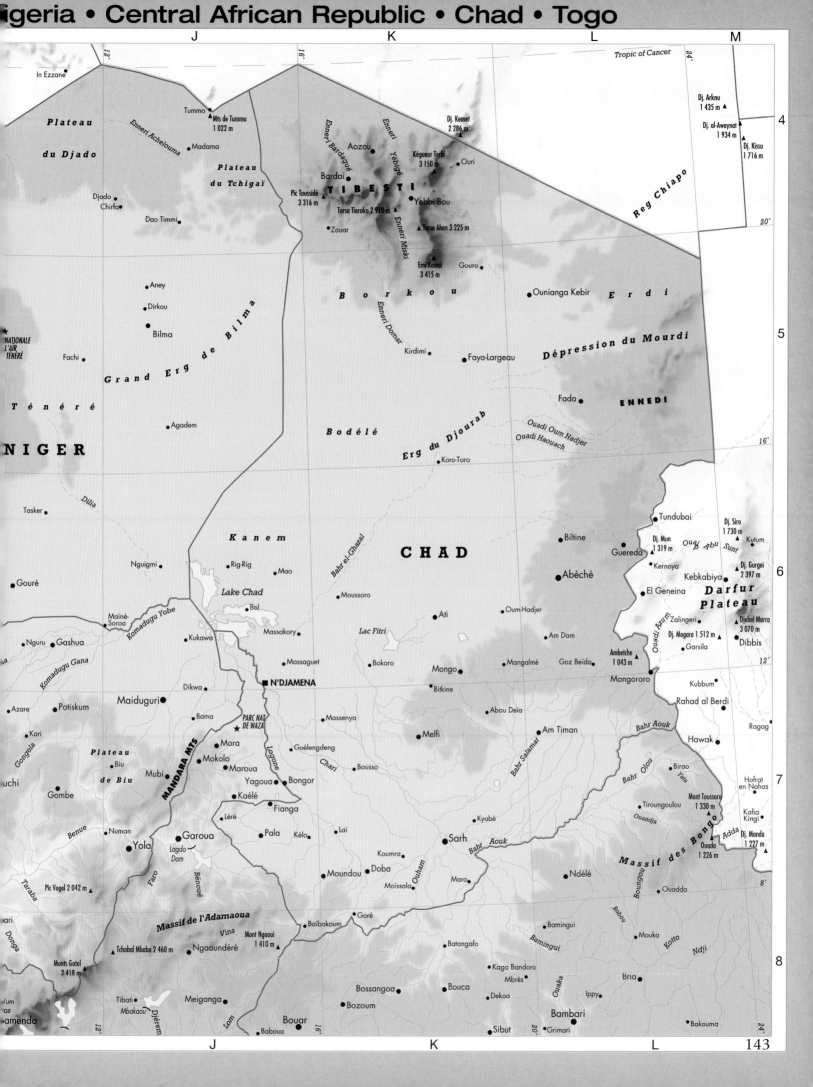

Map labels (as shown):

J   K   L   M

In Ezzane

Tropic of Cancer

Dj. Arknu 1 435 m ▲

Tummo ▲ Mts de Tummo 1 022 m
Dj. Kemet 2 286 m ▲
Dj. al-Awaynat 1 934 m ▲
Dj. Kissu 1 716 m ▲

Plateau du Djado
Madama •
Enneri Achelouma
Enneri Bardagué
Enneri Yébigé
Aozou •
Kégueur Terbi 3 150 m
Ouri •
Plateau du Tchigaï
Bardai •
T I B E S T I
Reg Chiapo

Djado •
Chirfa •
Pic Toussidé 3 316 m ▲
Yebbi Bou •
Tarso Tieroko 2 910 m ▲
Dao Timmi •
Zouar •
Enneri Miski
Tarso Ahon 3 225 m ▲

Emi Koussi 3 415 m ▲
Gouro •

B o r k o u
Aney •
Ounianga Kebir •
E r d i

Dirkou •
Enneri Domar
Bilma •

NATIONALE L'AIR TÉNÉRÉ
Fachi •
Kirdimi •
Faya-Largeau •
Dépression du Mourdi

Grand Erg de Bilma
Fada •
E N N E D I

T é n é r é
Agadem •
B o d é l é
Ouadi Oum Hadjer
Ouadi Haouach

N I G E R
Erg du Djourab
Koro-Toro •

Tasker •
Dilia
Tundubai •
Dj. Siro 1 730 m ▲

K a n e m
Biltine •
Dj. Mun 1 319 m ▲
Ouadi Abu Sunt
Kutum •

Gouré •
Nguigmi •
Rig-Rig •
Mao •
Guereda •
Kernoya •
Dj. Gurgei 2 397 m ▲

C H A D
Abéché •
El Geneina •
Kebkabiya •
Darfur Plateau

Lake Chad
Bol •
Moussoro •
Zalingeri •
Djebel Marra 3 070 m ▲

Maïné-Soroa
Kukawa •
Massakory •
Ati •
Oum-Hadjer •
Dj. Mogara 1 512 m ▲
Dibbis •

Nguru • Gashua •
Komadugu Yobe
Lac Fitri
Am Dam •
Garsila •

Komadugu Gana
Massaguet •
Bokoro •
Mongo •
Mangalmé •
Goz Beïda •
Ambetche 1 043 m ▲
Mongororo •

Azare •
Dikwa •
N'DJAMENA
Bitkine •
Kubbum •

Maiduguri •
Bama •
Abou Deïa •
Rahad al Berdi •

Potiskum •
PARC NAT DE WAZA ★
Massenya •
Am Timan •
Bahr Aouk
Ragag •

Kari •
Gongola
Mora •
Melfi •
Bahr Salamat
Bahr Olou •
Hawak •

Plateau de Biu
Biu •
Mokolo •
Guélengdeng •
Bousso •
Birao •
Hofrat en Nahas •

Mubi •
MANDARA MTS
Maroua •
Chari
Yaïa •

Gombe •
Yagoua •
Bongor •
Laï •
Kyabé •
Mont Toussoro 1 330 m ▲
Kafia Kingi •

Kaélé •
Fianga •
Tiroungoulou •
Ouandja •
Adda

Léré •
Pala •
Kélo •
Sarh •
Bahr Aouk
Ouada 1 226 m •
Dj. Manda 1 227 m ▲

Benue •
Numan •
Garoua •
Koumra •
Massif des Bongo

Yola •
Lagdo Dam
Moundou •
Doba •
Maro •
Ndélé •
Ouadda •

Pic Vogel 2 042 m ▲
Faro
Bénoué
Moïssala •

Taraba
Massif de l'Adamaoua
Baïbokoum •
Goré •
Bamingui •

Vina
Mont Ngaoui 1 410 m ▲
Batangafo •
Mouka •
Kotto
Ndji

Monts Gotel 2 418 m ▲
Tchabal Mbabo 2 460 m ▲
Ngaoundéré •
Kaga Bandoro •
Bria •

Donga
Tibati •
Meiganga •
Mbrés •
Ouaka
Ippy •

Mbakaou •
Djérem
Bossangoa •
Bouca •
Dekoa •
Bambari •

amenda
Baboua •
Bouar •
Bozoum •
Sibut •
Bakouma •
Grimari •

J   K   L

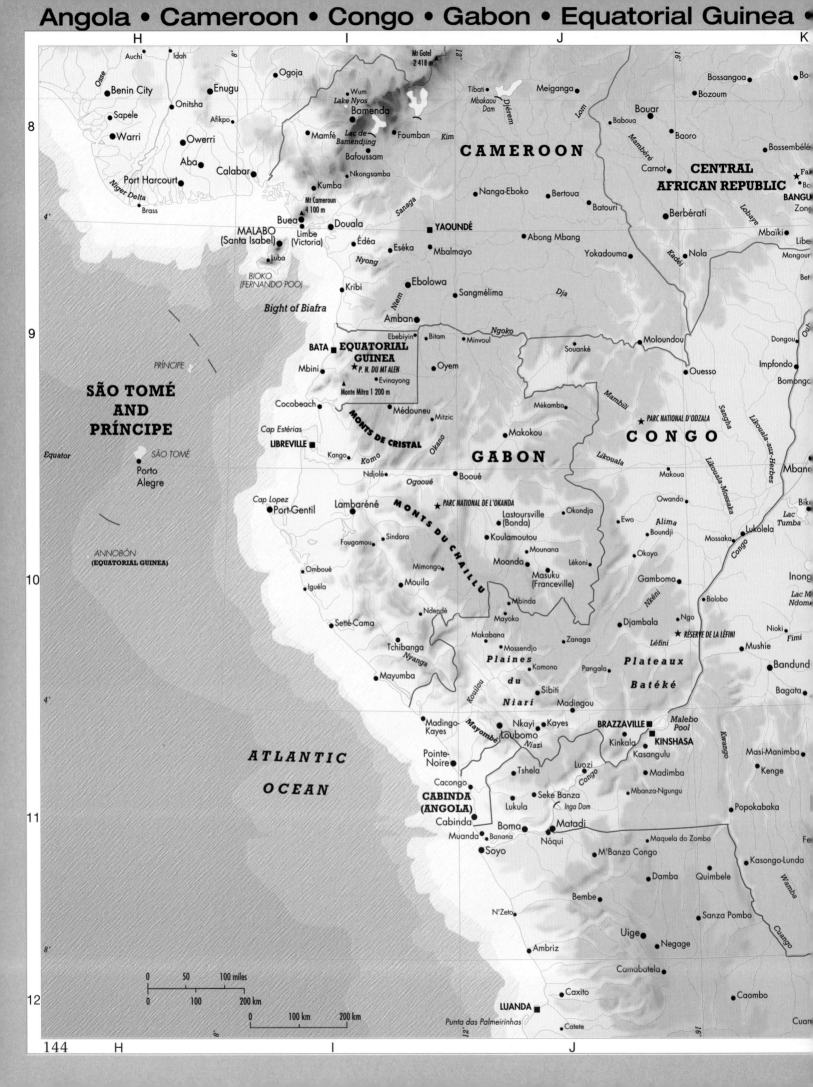

L 24° M 28° N 32° O

8

a Bandoro
Mbrés
Bria
Ippy
Bambari
Grimari
Bakouma
Kordango 830 m
Djema
Khogali
Tambura
Binza
Yei
Olo
Tapari
Amadi
Mongalla
Juba
Kidepo

ut
Kotto
Ouara
Obo
Mbomou
Doruma
Yambio
Maridi
Sue
Maridi
Yei
Moyo
Arua
Torit
Kinyeti
3 187 m
Nimule

Bangassou
Zemio
Asa
Banda
Uere
Dungu
Faradje
Nzoro
Watsa
Kibali

Mobaye
Ouango
Monga
Bili
Ango
Uele
Niangara
Dungu
Uele
Arua
Gulu
Aswa

Bosobolo
Yakoma
Bondo
Bomokandi
Poko
Isiro
Nepoko
Mungbere
Mahagi
Aburo 2 449 m
UGANDA
Lira

Businga
Abumombazi
Likati
Likati
Titule
Bima
Wamba
Mongbwalu
Bunia
Victoria Nile
Lake Kwania
Masindi

emena
Dua
Buta
Rubi
Babeyru
Nia-Nia
Ituri
Mambasa
Irumu
Lake Albert

Kungu
Budjala
Aketi
Mondjamboli
Itimbiri
Tele
Banalia
Lindi
Aruwimi
Beni
Butembo
Fort Portal
Muzizi
Mubende
KAMPALA
Entebbe
Équateur

Lisala
Bumba
Basoko
Yahuma
Isangi
Yangambi
Falls
Kisangani
Yatolema
Congo
Lindi
Margherita
5 109 m
Kasese
Lake George
Masaka
Lake Victoria

Bongandanga
Djolu
Bolombo
Mompono
Befori
Ubundu
Maiko
QUEEN ELIZABETH NATIONAL PARK
Mbarara
Kyaka

Boende
Opala
Lubutu
Lake Edward
Rutshuru
Kabale
Biharamulo
Geita

Ikela
Lomela
Punia
Walikale
Karisimbi 4 507 m
Nyiragongo
P. N. DES VIRUNGA
Goma
Gisenyi
Ruhengeri
KIGALI
Ngara

Monkoto
Luilaka
Lomela
DEMOCRATIC
Kalima
Shabunda
Kalehe
Bukavu
Cyangugu
RWANDA
Ngozi

Kiri
Lokoro
Congo Basin
REPUBLIC
Kindu
Pangi
Ulindi
Mwenga
Uvira
Gitega
Kibondo

Oshwe
Dekese
Lukénié
Kole
Lodja
Kataka-Kombe
OF CONGO
Elila
BUJUMBURA
BURUNDI

Ilebo
Bena Dibele
Sankuru
Kibamba
Kasongo
Luama
Kabambare
Kasulu
Kigoma
Ujiji
Uvinza

ungu
sanga
Mweka
Lubefu
Tshofa
Kongolo
TANZANIA

Kikwit
Luebo
Demba
Dimbelenge
Lukuga
Kabalo
Nyunzu
MONTS MAKARI
Kalemie
Sisaba 2 462 m
Mpanda

Gungu
Kananga
Mbuji-Mayi
Kabinda
Lomami
Kabongo
Kingombe
Luvua
Karema

Tshikapa
Kasumba
Tshimbulu
Dibaya
Gandajika
Muyumba
Manono
Moba
Kipili

Luiza
Lulua
Mwene Ditu
Bushimaie
Kaniama
MONTS MITUMBA
MONTS MUGILA
Lake Tanganyika

Lovua
Chitato
Lucapa
Chiumbe
Kasai
Malemba Nkulu
Pweto
MONTS MARUNGU
Kasanga
Mbala

unda
ateau
Caungula
Luangue
Kasai
Kamina
Lac Upemba
Mitwaba
MONTS KUNDELUNGU
Lake Mweru
Kilwa
Kasama

Sandoa
Lubudi
Bukama
Luena
Luvira
Luena
ZAMBIA
Kawamba

L 20° 24° M N 145

Angola • Democratic Republic of Congo

Madingo-Kayes
Nkayi
Kayes
BRAZZAVILLE
Malebo Pool
Ilebo
Mayombé
Loubomo
Niazi
Kinkala
KINSHASA
Bulungu
Mweka
Lusambo
Lubef
Pointe-Noire
Tshela
Luozi
Kasangulu
Madimba
Masi-Manimba
Lusanga
Luebo
Demba
Dimbelenge
Cacongo
Seke Banza
Inga Dam
Mbanza-Ngungu
Kenge
Kikwit
Kananga
Mbuji-Mayi
Kabind
CABINDA (ANGOLA)
Lukula
Popokabaka
Gungu
Kasumba
Tshimbulu
Cabinda
Boma
Matadi
Feshi
Tshikapa
Dibaya
Gand
Muanda
Banana
Nóqui
Maquela do Zombo
Kasongo-Lunda
Mwene Ditu
Soyo
M'Banza Congo
Damba
Quimbele
Kahemba
Lovua
Chitato
Luiza
Kaniama
Bembe
Sanza Pombo
Lunda Plateau
Chiumbe
Lucapa
N'Zeto
Uige
Negage
Caungula
Kapanga
Ambriz
Camabatela
Caombo
Cuango
Saurimo
Caxito
LUANDA
Punta das Palmeirinhas
Catete
Malanje
Capenda Camulemba
Sandoa
QUICAMA NATIONAL PARK
Dondo
Cuanza
Nova Gaia
Malonga
Kasaji
Dilolo
ANGOLA
Quibala
Luando
Lovua
Porto Amboim
Cuvo
Andulo
Cuanza
Luena
Cazombo
Sumbe
Camacupa
Munhango
CAMEIA NATIONAL PARK
Calunda
Lobito
Balombo
Huambo
Kuito (Bié)
Luena
Morro de Mocco 2 620 m
Chavuma
Benguela
Huambo
Cassamba
Zambezi
Dombe Grande
Ganda
Cuima
Chitembo
Muangangia
Cangamba
Luanguing
Lukul
Chissua 2 090 m
Caconda
Sessa
Lucira
Chicomba
Cunene
Cuchi
Menongue
Cuando
Chiume
Barotseland Plain
Lubango
Quipongo
Matala
Cassinga
Cuito Cuanavale
Mongu
Namibe
Serra da Chela
Caiundo
BICUARI NATIONAL PARK
Cahama
MUPA NATIONAL PARK
Cubango
ZAMBI
Tombua
Ponta da Marca
IONA NATIONAL PARK
Chitado
Ruacana
Xangongo
Ondjiva
Melunga
Cuangar
Mucusso
Caprivi Strip
Foz do Cunene
Ondangwa
Rundu
Shakawe
Opuwo
NAMIBIA
Omatako
Sepupa
BOTSWANA
Cape Fria
Namutoni
Tsumeb
Okavango Delta
Rocky Point
Etosha Pan
Okaukuejo
Nokaneng

50 100 miles
100 km 200 km
200

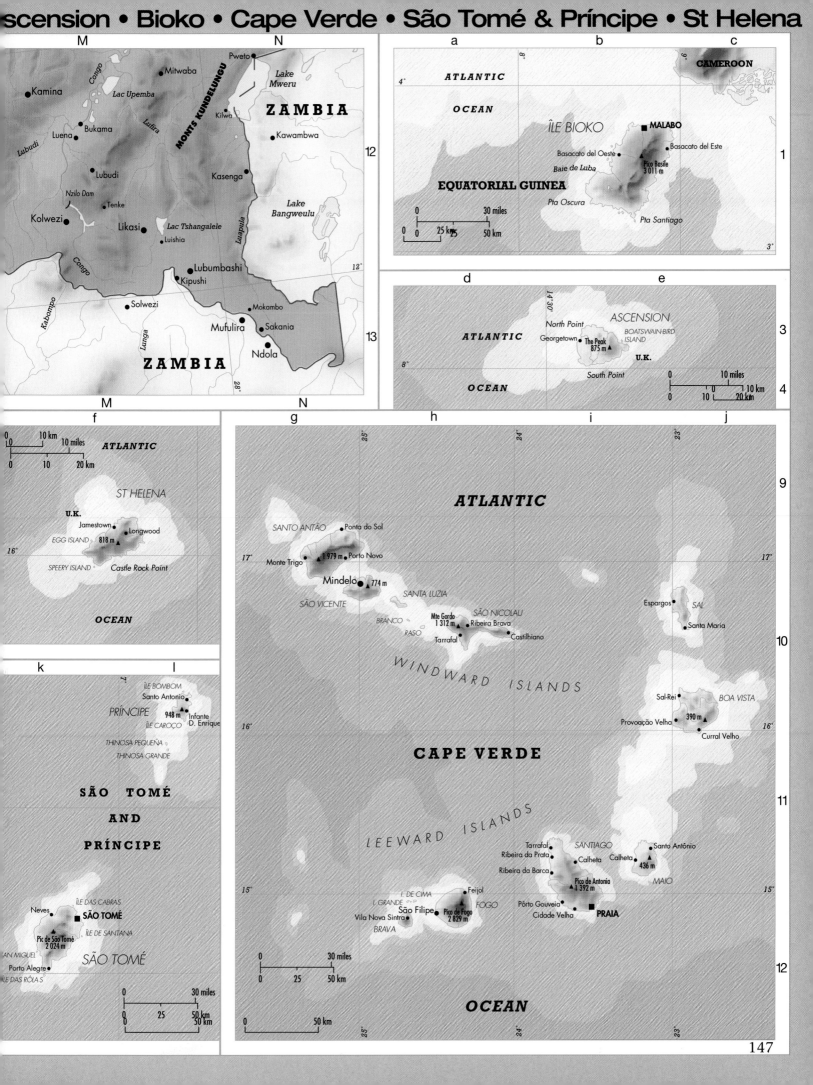

Map labels:

M N

Pweto
Mitwaba
Kamina
Congo
Lac Upemba
Luvua
Lufira
MONTS KUNDELUNGU
Kilwa
Lake Mweru
ZAMBIA
Bukama
Luena
Lubudi
Kawambwa
Lubudi
Kasenga
Nzilo Dam
Tenke
Kolwezi
Likasi
Lac Tshangalele
Luishia
Lake Bangweulu
Kabompo
Congo
Lunga
Luapula
Lubumbashi
Kipushi
Solwezi
Mokambo
Mufulira
Sakania
ZAMBIA
Ndola

12

13

M N

a b c

CAMEROON

ATLANTIC
OCEAN

ÎLE BIOKO
MALABO

Basacato del Oeste
Basacato del Este
Baie de Luba
Pico Basile
3 011 m

EQUATORIAL GUINEA

Pta Oscura
Pta Santiago

0   30 miles
0   25 km   50 km

1

d e

ASCENSION

North Point
BOATSWAIN-BIRD ISLAND
Georgetown
The Peak
875 m
ATLANTIC
U.K.
South Point
OCEAN

0   10 miles
0   10 km
0   10 20 km

3

4

f

0   10 km
0   10 miles
0   10 20 km

ATLANTIC

ST HELENA
U.K.
Jamestown
Longwood
EGG ISLAND
818 m
SPEERY ISLAND
Castle Rock Point

OCEAN

16

g h i j

ATLANTIC

SANTO ANTÃO
Ponta do Sol
Monte Trigo
1 979 m
Porto Novo
Mindelo
774 m
SÃO VICENTE
SANTA LUZIA
Mte Gordo
1 312 m
SÃO NICOLAU
Ribeira Brava
BRANCO
RASO
Tarrafal
Castilhiano

Espargos
SAL
Santa Maria

W I N D W A R D   I S L A N D S

Sal-Rei
BOA VISTA
Provoação Velha
390 m
Curral Velho

CAPE VERDE

L E E W A R D   I S L A N D S

Tarrafal
SANTIAGO
Santo Antônio
Ribeira da Prata
Calheta
Calheta
436 m
Ribeira da Barca
MAIO
Pico de Antonio
1 392 m
Feijol
I. DE CIMA
I. GRANDE
São Filipe
Pico de Fogo
2 829 m
FOGO
Pôrto Gouveia
Vila Nova Sintra
Cidade Velha
PRAIA
BRAVA

0   30 miles
0   25   50 km

9

17

10

16

11

15

12

k l

ÎLE BOMBOM
Santo Antonio
PRÍNCIPE
948 m
Infante D. Enrique
ÎLE CAROÇO
THINOSA PEQUEÑA
THINOSA GRANDE

S Ã O   T O M É

A N D

P R Í N C I P E

ÎLE DAS CABRAS
Neves
SÃO TOMÉ
ÎLE DE SANTANA
Pic de São Tomé
2 024 m
AN MIGUEL
Porto Alegre
SÃO TOMÉ
ÎLE DAS RÔLAS

0   30 miles
0   25   50 km

OCEAN

0   50 km

The countries of the region

The 24 countries of Central and West Africa range in size from the Democratic Republic of Congo, four times the size of France, to the tiny volcanic island outcrops of São Tomé and Príncipe, together smaller than the Greek island of Rhodes. Their landscapes vary from deserts in the north to rain forest in the south.

EQUATORIAL GUINEA
Capital: Malabo
Population: 510 000
Languages: Spanish, French,
Fang, other local languages
Currency: 1 CFA franc =
100 centimes

CAPE VERDE

SENEGAL

THE GAMBIA

GUINEA-BISSAU

GUINEA

SIERRA LEONE

IVORY COAST

LIBERIA

ANGOLA
Capital: Luanda
Population: 13.1 million
Languages: Portuguese,
Umbundu, Kumbundu and Kikongo
Currency: 1 kwanza = 100 lwei

BENIN
Capital: Porto-Novo
Population: 6.5 million
Languages: French, Fon, Ge
Currency: 1 CFA (Communauté financière africaine) franc = 100 centimes

BURKINA
Capital: Ouagadougou
Population: 12.6 million
Languages: French, Mossi
and other local languages
Currency: 1 CFA franc = 100 centimes

CAMEROON
Capital: Yaounde
Population: 15.7 million
Languages: French, English
and many local languages
Currency: 1 CFA franc = 100 centimes

CAPE VERDE
Capital: Praia
Population: 450 000
Languages: Portuguese
and Crioulo
Currency: 1 Cape Verdean escudo = 100 centavos

CENTRAL AFRICAN REPUBLIC
Capital: Bangui
Population: 3.8 million
Languages: French, Sangho
Currency: 1 CFA franc = 100 centimes

CHAD
Capital: N'Djamena
Population: 6.3 million
Languages: French, Arabic
and many local languages
Currency: 1 CFA franc = 100 centimes

CONGO
Capital: Brazzaville
Population: 3.6 million
Languages: French, Kikongo,
Lingala, local languages
Currency: 1 CFA franc = 100 centimes

DEMOCRATIC REPUBLIC OF CONGO
Capital: Kinshasa
Population: 51.2 million
Languages: French, Lingala and other local languages
Currency: 1 Congolese franc = 100 centimes

GABON
Capital: Libreville
Population: 1.3 million
Languages: French, Fang and
other local languages
Currency: 1 CFA franc = 100 centimes

THE GAMBIA
Capital: Banjul
Population: 1.3 millon
Languages: English, Wolof
and other local languages
Currency: 1 dalasi = 100 butut

GHANA
Capital: Accra
Population: 20.4 million
Languages: English and
many local languages
Currency: 1 cedi = 100 pesewas

GUINEA
Capital: Conakry
Population: 8.3 million
Languages: French, Soussou,
Manika, local languages
Currency: 1 Guinean franc = 100 centimes

GUINEA-BISSAU
Capital: Bissau
Population: 1.4 million
Languages: Portuguese,
Crioulo and local languages
Currency: 1 CFA franc = 100 centimes

IVORY COAST
Capital: Yamoussoukro
Population: 16.3 million
Languages: French and
many local languages
Currency: 1 CFA franc = 100 centimes

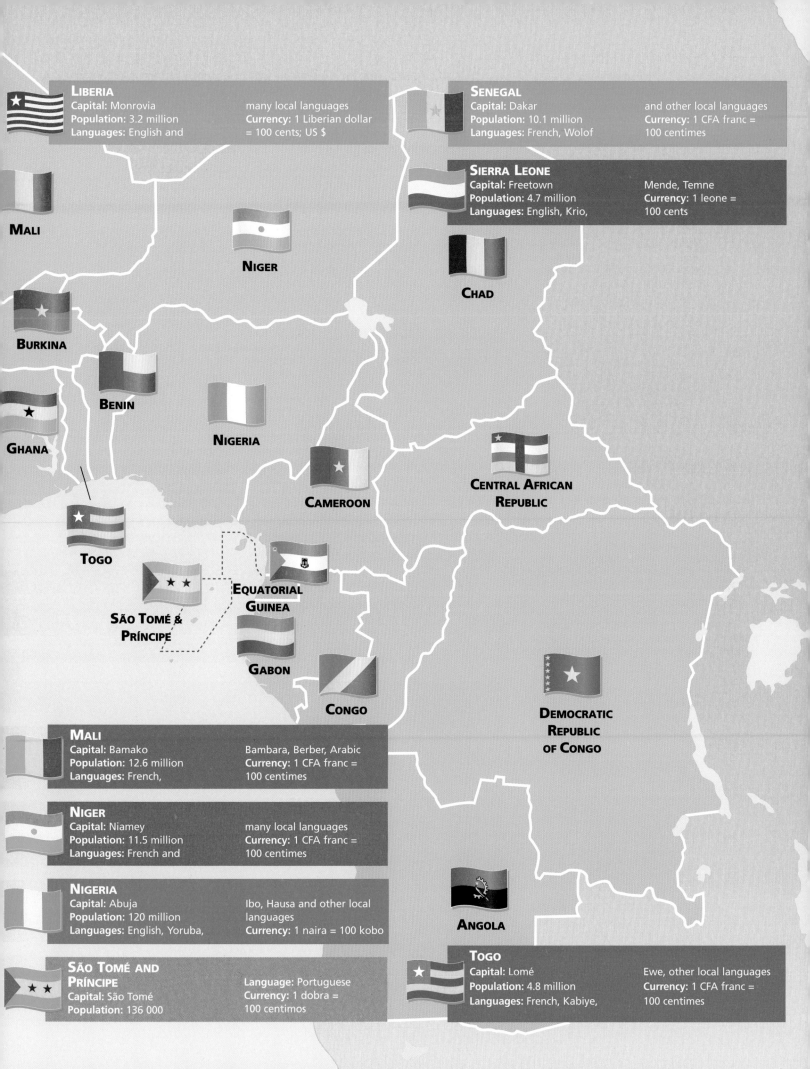

LIBERIA
Capital: Monrovia
Population: 3.2 million
Languages: English and
many local languages
Currency: 1 Liberian dollar
= 100 cents; US $

SENEGAL
Capital: Dakar
Population: 10.1 million
Languages: French, Wolof
and other local languages
Currency: 1 CFA franc =
100 centimes

SIERRA LEONE
Capital: Freetown
Population: 4.7 million
Languages: English, Krio,
Mende, Temne
Currency: 1 leone =
100 cents

MALI

NIGER

CHAD

BURKINA

BENIN

NIGERIA

GHANA

CAMEROON

CENTRAL AFRICAN REPUBLIC

TOGO

EQUATORIAL GUINEA

SÃO TOMÉ & PRÍNCIPE

GABON

CONGO

DEMOCRATIC REPUBLIC OF CONGO

MALI
Capital: Bamako
Population: 12.6 million
Languages: French,
Bambara, Berber, Arabic
Currency: 1 CFA franc =
100 centimes

NIGER
Capital: Niamey
Population: 11.5 million
Languages: French and
many local languages
Currency: 1 CFA franc =
100 centimes

NIGERIA
Capital: Abuja
Population: 120 million
Languages: English, Yoruba,
Ibo, Hausa and other local
languages
Currency: 1 naira = 100 kobo

ANGOLA

SÃO TOMÉ AND PRÍNCIPE
Capital: São Tomé
Population: 136 000
Language: Portuguese
Currency: 1 dobra =
100 centimos

TOGO
Capital: Lomé
Population: 4.8 million
Languages: French, Kabiye,
Ewe, other local languages
Currency: 1 CFA franc =
100 centimes

Climate, relief and vegetation

Heat is an inescapable fact of life in Central and West Africa, a region that lies entirely within the tropics. Mountains and high plains rise fairly abruptly from a narrow coastal strip, and the vegetation includes desert, semidesert, savannah grasslands, mangroves and tropical forests.

Hot and dry or hot and wet

Rainfall is highest around the Equator. The trade winds of the Northern and Southern Hemispheres meet, bringing together dry air from off the land and humid air from off the oceans.

This Inter-Tropical Convergence Zone (ITCZ) is an area of dense clouds and frequent thunderstorms. Parts of the Congo basin have more than 79 in (2000 mm) of rain a year. Rainfall in the equatorial zone is fairly consistent through the year. Farther from the Equator, there are wet and dry seaons, and the rainy season becomes shorter and the rainfall lower, even during the rainy months. This 'wet and dry' climate helps to create the savannah regions, which in the north merge into the semi-arid Sahel, then the Sahara.

In winter, the *harmattan*, a hot wind blowing off the Sahara, brings hot, dry weather to West Africa. Apart from its dryness, the climate of the desert is marked by huge temperature swings, of more than 30°C (54°F), between daytime and night-time.

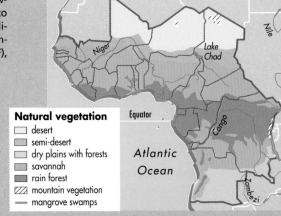

Natural vegetation
- ☐ desert
- semi-desert
- ☐ dry plains with forests
- savannah
- rain forest
- ▨ mountain vegetation
- — mangrove swamps

Cape Verde, the struggle with drought

Water shortage, leading to crop failure and famine, is never far off for the people of Cape Verde. A combination of low rainfall, frequent droughts and rugged terrain means that only 10 per cent of the islands' land surface can be cultivated to grow staple crops, such as maize, cassava and beans, and cash crops, including sugar cane and bananas. Elsewhere, the islanders raise livestock on dry, scrubby pastures. Since independence in 1975, governments have made huge efforts to face the problem. They have built desalination plants, sunk wells and constructed thousands of small dams and dykes to catch the rain that does fall. They have also planted millions of drought-resistant trees on the islands' bare volcanic mountainsides.

AVERAGE TEMPERATURES		
	January	July
Abidjan	27°C (81°F)	26°C (79°C)
Bamako	23°C (73°F)	27°C (81°F)
Bangui	26°C (79°C)	25°C (77°F)
Dakar	24°C (75°F)	27°C (81°F)
Kinshasa	26°C (79°C)	22°C (72°F)
Luanda	27°C (81°F)	21°C (70°F)
Monrovia	26°C (79°C)	24°C (75°F)
N'Djamena	23°C (73°F)	28°C (82°F)
Niamey	23°C (73°F)	29°C (84°F)
Yaoundé	24°C (75°F)	22°C (72°F)

Water highway A dugout canoe on the Sénégal river. Like the Niger, the Sénégal rises in the Fouta Djallon highlands, but then turns west, rather than east, towards the Atlantic.

AVERAGE RAINFALL (inches/mm)			
	Total	Wettest month	Driest month
Abidjan	84.6/2146	24.0/610 (June)	1.0/26 (March)
Bamako	38.5/976	11.0/280 (Aug)	0 (Feb)
Bangui	61.3/1555	8.9/225 (Aug)	0.8/20 (Jan)
Dakar	19.7/499	7.3/185 (Aug)	0 (Feb)
Kinshasa	54.6/1385	9.3/235 (Nov)	0.04/1 (July)
Luanda	14.7/374	4.9/125 (April)	0 (July)
Monrovia	202.3/5135	39.2/995 (July)	1.2/30 (Jan)
N'Djamena	23.6/599	8.5/215 (Aug)	0 (Jan)
Niamey	23.8/603	7.9/200 (Aug)	0 (Dec)
Yaoundé	60.8/1542	11.8/300 (Oct)	0.8/20 (Dec)

WHERE THE SUN SHINES (hours per year)	
	Total
Abidjan	2108
Bamako	2733
Bangui	2061
Dakar	3090
Kinshasa	1692
Luanda	2330
Monrovia	1991
N'Djamena	3122
Niamey	3226
Yaoundé	1627

A continent of plains and plateaus

Africa stretches around 5000 miles (8000 km) from Tunisia's Cap Bon in the north to the Cape of Good Hope in the south, and for the most part it is relatively flat: the continent's underlying rock platform is exceptionally old and has been worn down during the course of billions of years. Its most imposing mountain ranges are confined to the edges – the Atlas Mountains in the north and the Cape ranges in the south. Elsewhere, the stresses and strains of the Earth's crust have created the spectacular gash of the Rift Valley, marking the eastern edge of Central Africa, and volcanic mountains, such as Mount Cameroon. Rising from inland plateaus, occasional outcrops known as inselbergs – literally 'island mountains' – are all that survive of earlier rock layers, elsewhere eroded. Narrow coastal plains fringe the continent, dropping to equally narrow offshore continental shelves.

From rain forest to desert

The rain forests of the equatorial region are notable for the astonishing diversity of their wildlife. Trees with shallow roots reach heights of 164 ft (50 m). Beneath them are packed other layers – populated with smaller trees, tree ferns and epiphytes (plants, such as orchids, that grow on other plants) – each adapted to different levels of sunlight and shade. Farther away from the Equator, the tree cover becomes more dispersed. As the climate becomes drier, savannah grasslands take over, at first quite thickly wooded and with tall grasses, then more scrubby and with shorter grasses. The few shrubs that survive in the desert put down deep roots to tap any available water. Plants germinate within days of rare rainfall, and complete their life cycle within two weeks or less.

River waterways

Africa's second-longest river, the Congo, is the world's eighth-longest. Even its minor tributaries would pass for mighty rivers in Europe. Its remotest source, the Chambeshi, rises in the mountains of northern Zambia; its largest, in terms of water volume, is the Lualaba, which rises in the Shaba highlands of south-eastern Congo-Kinshasa. The Congo makes a huge counterclockwise arc through Central Africa before tumbling down the 32 cataracts of the Livingstone (or Inga) Falls and into the Atlantic. To the north, the Niger is the continent's third-longest river, rising in the Fouta Djallon highlands of Guinea, then forming an arc through West Africa and into the Gulf of Guinea in Nigeria.

Despite their majestic size, neither river is fully navigable: rapids, such as the Congo's Livingstone Falls, form barriers that prevent oceangoing ships from reaching far inland. In the deserts and the semideserts, many rivers are endoreic – they never reach the sea, but flow into lakes, such as Lake Chad, that form in depressions. The deserts are also crisscrossed with *wadis* water courses that are dry most of the time, but can turn suddenly into raging torrents when rain falls.

HIGHEST PEAKS	
(altitude in ft/m)	
Margherita Peak (Congo-Kinshasa/Uganda)	16 794/5119
Mt Karisimbi (Congo-Kinshasa/Rwanda)	14 787/4507
Mt Cameroon (Cameroon)	13 451/4100
Emi Koussi (Chad)	11 204/3415
Pico de Fogo (Cape Verde)	9281/2829
Morro de Môco (Angola)	8599/2620
Dimlang/Vogel Peak (Nigeria)	6699/2042
Pico de São Tomé (São Tomé & Príncipe)	6640/2024

FOREST AREA	
(percentage of total area)	
Gabon	81.5
Congo-Brazzaville	64.5
Equatorial Guinea	62.5
Congo-Kinshasa	60.9
Guinea-Bissau	60.5
Cameroon	50.2
Cen. African Republic	36.8
Senegal	31.5
Liberia	31.2
São Tomé & Príncipe	28.1
Ghana	26.6
Benin	23.5

RIVERS	
(length in miles/km)	
Congo	2900/4700
Niger	2600/4200
Sénégal	1020/1640
Volta	1000/1600
Chari	870/1400
Gambia	700/1120

Bridge in the trees
A rope bridge in the rain forest of Cameroon. Timber accounts for 10 per cent of the country's exports.

Population, economy and society

The population of Central and West Africa in 2002 was estimated at more than 331 million. Across the region as a whole, just under 60 per cent of people still lived in the countryside. But there were significant variations from country to country. Burkina had the highest rural population – 83 per cent. Its mirror image was Gabon, the most urban society, where 82 per cent of the people lived in towns and cities.

Africa and AIDS

Out of an estimated 3 million people who died worldwide of AIDS in 2001, 2.2 million came from sub-Saharan Africa. AIDS is currently the continent's biggest killer – well ahead of older scourges such as malaria. According to the World Health Organisation, 3.5 million Africans were infected with HIV/AIDS during 2001, bringing the continent's total number of sufferers to 28.5 million. The average life expectancy in sub-Saharan Africa is 47; it is estimated that it would be 62 without AIDS. In fact, Central and West Africa have escaped relatively lightly – in Nigeria, for example, 5.8 per cent of the adult population are infected, compared with nearly 34 per cent in Zimbabwe.

WHERE PEOPLE LIVE ▼

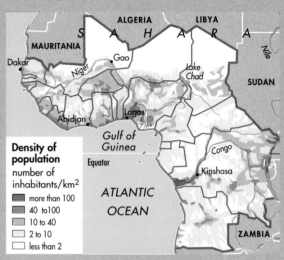

Density of population
number of inhabitants/km²
- more than 100
- 40 to 100
- 10 to 40
- 2 to 10
- less than 2

LIFE EXPECTANCY

	Men	Women
Angola	43	46
Benin	51	55
Burkina	44	46
Cameroon	49	50
Cape Verde	64	71
Central African Republic	42	46
Chad	43	46
Congo (Brazzaville)	48	53
Congo (Dem. Rep.)	49	52
Equatorial Guinea	48	51
Gabon	51	53
The Gambia	44	46
Ghana	55	57
Guinea	46	47
Guinea-Bissau	42	45
Ivory Coast	47	48
Liberia	47	49
Mali	49	51
Niger	44	44
Nigeria	51	51
São Tomé & Príncipe	67	67
Senegal	50	54
Sierra Leone	36	38
Togo	50	52

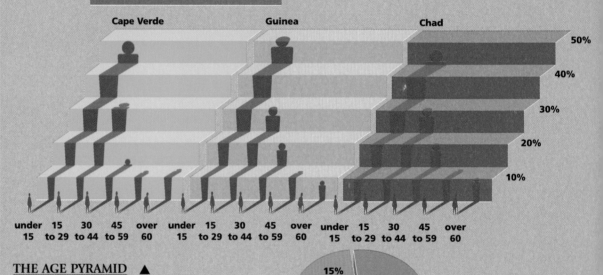

THE AGE PYRAMID ▲

ETHNIC COMPOSITION OF CAMEROON, GABON AND IVORY COAST ▶

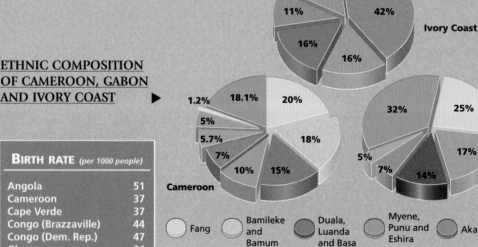

INFANT MORTALITY
(deaths per 1000 live births)

Angola	118
Cameroon	79
Cape Verde	50
Congo (Brazzaville)	66
Congo (Dem. Rep.)	77
Ghana	62
Niger	126
Nigeria	78
Senegal	57
Sierra Leone	146

BIRTH RATE *(per 1000 people)*

Angola	51
Cameroon	37
Cape Verde	37
Congo (Brazzaville)	44
Congo (Dem. Rep.)	47
Ghana	34
Niger	55
Nigeria	41
Senegal	39
Sierra Leone	49

TRADING (IMPORTS AND EXPORTS) OF IVORY COAST, BURKINA, BENIN AND NIGERIA
(in millions of US dollars, 2002) ▼

577 165

7547

15 107

Burkina

2613   3851

651   360

Benin

Ivory Coast

Nigeria

DISTRIBUTION OF THE WORKING POPULATION ▼

Human development

Central and West Africa fares bleakly in the United Nations' Human Development Index. This measures countries' human (as opposed to purely economic) development, combining statistics for life expectancy, education and adult literacy as well as gross domestic product per head.
At 173rd, Sierra Leone ranks last in the world – behind Niger at 172nd, Burkina at 169th and Chad at 166th. Oil-rich Equatorial Guinea and Gabon do better at 111th and 117th. Ranking highest in the region is Cape Verde, 100th in the world. Life expectancy figures – just under 70 – are comparable to those in parts of Europe.

SERVICE INDUSTRIES
Angola: 18.4%
Burkina: 6.3%
Cape Verde: 43.7%
Central African Republic: 19.2%
Liberia: 25%
Niger: 6.6%

MINING AND MANUFACTURING
Angola: 8.3%
Burkina: 1.2%
Cape Verde: 28.5%
Central African Republic: 3.8%
Liberia: 5.2%
Niger: 4.3%

AGRICULTURE
Angola: 73.3%
Burkina: 92.5%
Cape Verde: 27.8%
Central African Republic: 76.9%
Liberia: 69.7%
Niger: 89.1%

GROSS DOMESTIC PRODUCT PER CAPITA
(in US dollars, 2002) ▼

Equatorial Guinea
4490

Gabon
3698

Cape Verde
1347

Liberia
1106

Cameroon
648

Ivory Coast
632

Senegal
482

Angola
396

Chad
210

Niger
175

Working together in Togo

Many Togolese farmers belong to grassroots cooperative associations known as *groupements*. These may have anything between 3 and 20 members, who work both as individuals on their own farms and collectively.
  Harvesting the crop is usually a collective activity. The crops are shared out fairly among the farmers and the collective sells the surplus, putting the profits into a members' fund. The cooperatives also have an educational and training role. Through them traditional farming and craft skills can be passed on, as well as up-to-date scientific information.

The dangers of overfishing

The seas off West Africa include some of the world's richest fishing grounds, and for the coastal peoples, fishing is a vital part of their life – up to 75 per cent of their protein comes from fish. In recent years, however, overfishing has resulted in a depletion of stocks.

For years, West African governments earned money by selling licences for European fleets to fish their territorial waters. But European factory trawlers were taking fish at unsustainable levels. The dugout canoes of modern African fishermen are more sophisticated than those of their forebears: they are large enough for a crew of 15, carry iceboxes and can stay at sea for two weeks. Even so, they are finding it harder to catch enough fish.

In 2001, Senegal refused to renew a fishing agreement with the European Union unless certain conditions were met – for example, about rest periods to allow stocks to renew themselves. When a deal was finally struck in June 2002, Senegal had won concessions, including an increased payment of 64 million euros for four years' fishing rights. It remains to be seen whether the new agreement will be enough to preserve the endangered stocks.

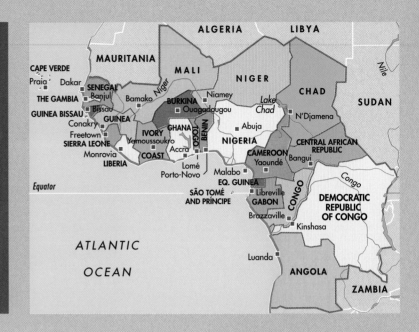

CONURBATIONS
(in thousand inhabitants, 2002 est.)

Lagos	10 000.0
Kinshasa	4885.0
Abidjan	3199.0
Ibadan	3078.4
Dakar	2104.0
Luanda	2550.0
Accra	1904.0
Conakry	1764.0
Douala	1239.1
Monrovia	479.0

Lagos, African megalopolis

Nigeria's largest city and economic and business capital, Lagos, is growing uncontrollably. From a population of 6000 in 1800, it grew to 280,000 in 1871, to 2.5 million in 1973, and an estimated 10 million today. Some 300,000 extra people move into the city each year. Its streets are a more or less permanent traffic jam; the luxurious modern office and apartment blocks of the centre contrast glaringly with the slums and shantytowns that mushroom round the city. Although Lagos has a thriving cultural life, it is also reckoned to be the dirtiest and most expensive city in Africa, as well as lying at the hub of the continent's trade in hard drugs.

When the traffic stopped *Yet another traffic snarl-up brings downtown Lagos to a halt.*

A new partnership in Africa

In March 2002, the leaders of 21 African countries, meeting in Nigeria, endorsed a New Partnership for Africa's Development (Nepad). The plan was chiefly the work of five heads of state: the presidents of South Africa, Senegal, Nigeria, Algeria and Egypt. Nepad declared itself to be 'anchored on the determination of Africans to extricate themselves and the continent from the malaise of underdevelopment and exclusion in a globalising world'. It included commitments to more open government and better economic management. It also put the case for a huge increase in Western aid and investment. In June 2002, it was presented to the G8 summit of the world's richest nations. The G8 gave asssurances of increased aid and promised to reconsider trade barriers and farm subsidies that made it hard for African products to compete on world markets.

Nigeria
955 000

Ghana
439 000

Senegal
389 000

Ivory Coast
301 000

Gabon
169 000

Benin
152 000

Burkina
126 000

The Gambia
96 000

Cameroon
59 000

Sierra Leone
24 000

◀ TOURISM *(number of visitors per year)*

Index

Page numbers in *italics* denote illustrations. The letter and number references in brackets are the co-ordinates for places in the map section, pp. 140-7.

Acknowledgments

Abbreviations: t = top m = middle, b = bottom, l = left, r = right.

FRONT COVER: *The ruins of Djaba, east of Ténéré (Niger)*:
HOA QUI/J. Hagenmuller
BACK COVER: *Bus stop*: HOA QUI/O. Martel

4/5: COSMOS/P. Maitre; 6: COSMOS/SPL/Planetary Visions/Geosphere Project-T. van Sant; 8t, b: ALTITUDE/Y. Arthus-Bertrand; 9r: HOA QUI/J.-L. Manaud; 10l: BIOS/M. Laboureur; 10r: BIOS/F.N.H./Gunther; 11t: BIOS/N. Granier; 12t: HOA QUI/S. Grandadam; 12b: ALTITUDE/Y. Arthus-Bertrand; 13r: EXPLORER/G. Philippart de Foy; 14l: COSMOS/P. Maitre; 14r: HOA QUI/M. Denis-Huot; 15t: HOA QUI/M. Marenthier; 16t: COSMOS/F. Perri; 16b: EXPLORER/G. Bosio; 17r: ALTITUDE/F. Vezia; 18bl: HOA QUI/M. Huet; 18bm, br: B. NANTET; 19t: HOA QUI/M. Ascani; 19b: COSMOS/Steinmetz; 20tl: B. NANTET; 20tr: EXPLORER/G. Philippart de Foy; 20m, b: B. NANTET; 21r: CORBIS-SYGMA/N. Wheeler; 21b: B. NANTET; 22tl: B. NANTET/Museum of Ifé, Nigeria; 22tr: RMN/J.-G. Berizzi/Musée des Arts d'Afrique et d'Océanie, Paris; 22b: RMN/CFAO/Labat/Musée des Arts d'Afrique et d'Océanie, Paris; 23t: HOA QUI/F. Michele; 23b: GAMMA/M. Deville; 24t: COSMOS/P. Maitre; 24b: RMN/J.-G. Berizzi; 25t: EXPLORER/GEOPRESS; 25b: ALTITUDE/Y. Arthus-Bertrand; 26tl: CORBIS-SYGMA/Archivo Iconográfico, S. A.; 26tr, bl, bm: B. NANTET; 26br: CORBIS-SYGMA/Hulton Deutsch Collection; 27: CORBIS-SYGMA/Bettmann Archive; 28t: COSMOS/G. Buthaud; 28b: GAMMA/R. Job; 29t: CORBIS-SYGMA/Bettmann Archive; 29br: GAMMA/Y. Latronche; 30/31: COSMOS/F. Perri; 32: BIOS/G. Nicolet; 34l: COSMOS/Steinmetz; 34r: ALTITUDE/Y. Arthus-Bertrand; 35t: HOA QUI/M. Ascani; 35m: HOA QUI/Ph. Bourseiller; 36t: COSMOS/AURORA/R. Caputo; 36m, b: RAPHO/G. Gerster; 37t: HOA QUI/Y. Gellie; 37b: RAPHO/G. Gerster; 38t: ALTITUDE/F. Lechenet; 38b: ALTITUDE/M. Lavaud; 39t: HOA QUI/M. Marenthier; 39br: HOA QUI/M. Renaudeau; 40-45: ALTITUDE/Y. Arthus-Bertrand; 40t: HOA QUI/J.-L. Manaud; 40m: HOA QUI/J. Jaffre; 40b: HOA QUI/J.-L. Manaud; 41t: COSMOS/FOCUS/G. Menn; 41m: HOA QUI/J.-L. Manaud; 41bl: HOA QUI/A. Wolf; 41br: COSMOS/P. Maitre; 42t: ALTITUDE/Y. Arthus-Bertrand; 42b: COSMOS/P. Maitre; 43t: HOA QUI/M. Renaudeau; 43m: COSMOS/AURORA/M. Staber; 43bl: ALTITUDE/Y. Arthus-Bertrand; 43br: COSMOS/AURORA/M. Staber; 44tl: COSMOS/P. Maitre; 44tr: COSMOS/AURORA/M. Staber; 44mr, br: ALTITUDE/Y. Arthus-Bertrand; 45t, mt: HOA QUI/J.-L. Manaud; 45mb: COSMOS/AURORA/M. Staber; 45b: EXPLORER/P. Le Floc'h; 46t: HOA QUI/X. Richer; 46b: ALTITUDE/Y. Arthus-Bertrand; 47r: EXPLORER/C. Boutin; 48t: HOA QUI/M. Renaudeau; 48b: ALTITUDE/Y. Arthus-Bertrand; 49: COSMOS/AURORA/R. Caputo; 50t: BIOS/G. Nicolet; 50b: BIOS/R. Seitre; 51t: BIOS/M. Harvey; 51b: BIOS/M. Gunther; 52t: BIOS/M. & C. Denis-Huot; 52m: BIOS/M. Laboureur; 52b: HOA QUI/M. Renaudeau; 53tl: BIOS/T. Crocetta; 53tr: BIOS/R. Du Toit; 53m: BIOS/F. N. H./Gunther; 53b: BIOS/M. & C. Denis-Huot; 54: HOA QUI/D. Laine; 55t: COSMOS/F. Perri; 55m: COSMOS/P. Maitre; 55b: HOA QUI/J.-L. Manaud; 57t: HOA QUI/M. Renaudeau; 57m: COSMOS/F. Perri; 57b: EXPLORER/P. Bordes; 58t: HOA QUI/M. Ascani; 58m: COSMOS/D. Lainé; 58b: HOA QUI; 59: COSMOS/F. Perri; 59m: ALTITUDE/Y. Arthus-Bertrand; 59br: HOA QUI/E. Valentin; 60l: HOA QUI/J.-L. Manaud; 60r: HOA QUI/O. Martel; 61t: COSMOS/D. Lainé; 61br: HOA QUI/M. Renaudeau; 62t: HOA QUI/O. Martel; 62m: HOA QUI/J.-l. Lenée; 62b: HOA QUI/S. Grandadam; 63t: COSMOS/H. Bamberger; 63br: COSMOS/F. Perri; 64t, b: HOA QUI/M. Renaudeau; 65tr, m: HOA QUI/O. Martel; 65b: COSMOS/D. Lainé; 66t: COSMOS/F. Perri; 66bl: COSMOS/D. Lainé; 66br: COSMOS/ANZENBERGER/O. Mattioli; 67t: COSMOS/D. Lainé; 67br, 68l: COSMOS/P. Maitre; 68r:

EXPLORER/S. Frances; 69t: COSMOS/P. Maitre; 69br: HOA QUI/O. Martel; 70t: COSMOS/F. Perri; 70m: COSMOS/D. Lainé; 70b: HOA QUI/O. Martel; 71t: COSMOS/AURORA/J. Azel; 71bl: HOA QUI/M. Huet; 71br: HOA QUI/J.-L. Manaud; 72t: HOA QUI/M. Ascani; 72bl: HOA QUI/M. Renaudeau; 72br: HOA QUI/M. Denis-Huot; 73t: COSMOS/AURORA/R. Caputo; 73bl: EXPLORER/O. Riffet; 73br: HOA QUI/G. Boutin; 74: HOA QUI/E. Valentin; 76t: HOA QUI/P. Morel; 76b: ALTITUDE/Y. Arthus-Bertrand; 77t: HOA QUI/M. Renaudeau; 77m: COSMOS/AURORA/J. Azel; 77b: COSMOS/A. Keler; 78t, b: HOA QUI/M. Renaudeau; 79t, m: COSMOS/F. Perri; 79b: HOA QUI/C. Pavard; 80t: HOA QUI/M. Renaudeau; 80m: COSMOS/F. Perri; 80b: HOA QUI/M. Renaudeau; 81t: HOA QUI/M. Ascani; 81b: HOA QUI/C. Pavard; 82: ALTITUDE/Y. Arthus-Bertrand; 84t: HOA QUI/N. Thibaut; 84bl: COSMOS/B. & C. Alexander; 85t: HOA QUI/M. Renaudeau; 85m: COSMOS/P. Maitre; 85b: ALTITUDE/Y. Arthus-Bertrand; 86t: HOA QUI/C. Pavard; 86m: HOA QUI/P. Waeles; 86b: COSMOS/P. Maitre; 87t: COSMOS/F. Perri; 87m, b: HOA QUI/M. Renaudeau; 88t: HOA QUI/E. Valentin; 88bl: HOA QUI/C. Pavard; 88br: HOA QUI/M. Renaudeau; 89tl: HOA QUI/O. Martel; 89tr: EXPLORER/P. Lissac; 89br: COSMOS/AURORA/J. Azel; 90t: HOA QUI/G. Boutin; 90bl: ALTITUDE/Y. Arthus-Bertrand; 90br: COSMOS/P. Maitre; 91t: HOA QUI/J.-L. Manaud; 91b: COSMOS/P. Maitre; 92t: COSMOS/F. Perri; 92bl: HOA QUI/M. Renaudeau; 92br: HOA QUI/O. Martel; 93t: COSMOS/AURORA/R. Caputo; 93br: HOA QUI/B. Perousse; 94t: COSMOS/E. Ounand; 94bl: HOA QUI/M. Huet; 94br: HOA QUI/O. Martel; 95t: COSMOS/P. Maitre; 95m: COSMOS/VISUM/W. Bteche; 95br: COSMOS/P. Maitre; 96t: COSMOS/Steinmetz; 96m: EXPLORER/S. Frances; 96b: COSMOS/Steinmetz; 97t, m: COSMOS/F. Perri; 97b: HOA QUI/E. Valentin; 98t: HOA QUI/M. Marenthier; 98bl: HOA QUI/J.-L. Manaud; 98br: COSMOS/F. Perri; 99t: HOA QUI/M. Ascani; 99bl: HOA QUI/M. Renaudeau; 99br: HOA QUI/M. Huet; 100: HOA QUI/G. Bernard; 102t, m: HOA QUI/M. Renaudeau; 102b: COSMOS/F. Perri; 103t, b: GAMMA/Ph. Boudin; 104t: COSMOS/F. Perri; 104m: HOA QUI/P. Duval; 104b: HOA QUI/N. Thibaut; 105t: HOA QUI/C. Vaisse; 105m: COSMOS/G. Buthaud; 105b: HOA QUI/J.-L. Manaud; 106t, b: HOA QUI/N. Thibaut; 107t: HOA QUI/M. Renaudeau; 107m: EXPLORER/J. Brun; 107b: HOA QUI/M. Ascani; 108t: GAMMA/R. Job; 108bl: GAMMA/LIAISON/M. Linton; 108bm: GAMMA/LIAISON/Utsumi; 108br: GAMMA/K. Daher; 109t: COSMOS/H. Bamberger; 109bl, br: COSMOS/F. Perri; 110t: HOA QUI/O. Martel; 110b: HOA QUI/M. Ascani; 111t: COSMOS/D. Lainé; 111b: ALTITUDE/Y. Arthus-Bertrand; 112t: GAMMA/M. Deville; 112m, b: COSMOS/D. Lainé; 113t: GAMMA/LIAISON/Stone; 113bl: HOA QUI/M. Renaudeau; 113br: EXPLORER/G. Philippart de Foy; 114t: COSMOS/F. Perri; 114m: EXPLORER/S. Frances; 114b: COSMOS/F. Perri; 115t: COSMOS/P. Maitre; 115b: ALTITUDE/Y. Arthus-Bertrand; 116t: COSMOS/Steinmetz; 116m: GAMMA/A. Ribeiro; 116b: COSMOS/IMPACT/G. Hoberly; 117t: COSMOS/Steinmetz; 117br: HOA QUI/M. Renaudeau; 118t: COSMOS/Steinmetz; 118b: ALTITUDE/P. Bourseiller; 119t: COSMOS/F. Perri; 119m: GAMMA/G. Merillon; 119b: COSMOS/F. Perri; 120t: COSMOS/P. Maitre; 120bl, br: HOA QUI/M. Ascani; 121t: COSMOS/F. Perri; 121b: COSMOS/P. Maitre; 122t: AFP/D. Minkoh; 122b: COSMOS/P. Maitre; 123t, b: GAMMA/C. Poulet; 124t: GAMMA/P. Aventurier; 124bl: HOA QUI/M. Renaudeau; 124br: RAPHO/D. Riffet; 125t: GAMMA/R. Job; 125m: HOA QUI/M. Renaudeau; 125b: ALTITUDE/M. Lavaud; 126t: GAMMA/LIAISON/Linton; 126bl: COSMOS/AURORA/J. Azel; 126br: COSMOS/AURORA/R. Caputo; 127t:

COSMOS/JB PICTURES/J.-L. Gubb; 127m, b: HOA QUI/G. Bernard; 128: HOA QUI/M. Renaudeau; 130t: HOA QUI/Treal-Ruiz; 130bl: GAMMA/A. Buu; 130br: EXPLORER/C. Lenars; 131m: GAMMA/C. Ducasse; 131b: HOA QUI/M. Renaudeau; 132t: EXPLORER/S. Frances; 132bl: GAMMA/X. Rossi; 132br: RAPHO/E. Luider; 133t, b: GAMMA/C. Lepetit; 134t: GAMMA/J.-M. Loubat; 134bl: RMN/J.-G. Berizzi; 134br: HOA QUI/M. Renaudeau; 135t: RAPHO/D. Riffet; 135bl: HOA QUI/M. Renaudeau; 135br: COSMOS/ANZENBERGER/G. Thome; 136t: RMN/Arnaudet; 136m: GAMMA/P. Maitre; 136b: AFP/Seyllou; 137tl: GAMMA/M. Pelletier; 137tr: GAMMA/Y. Latronche; 137b: GAMMA/Satelight; 138/139: GAMMA/M. Deville; 150: COSMOS/F. Perri; 151: BIOS/G. Nicolet; 154: COSMOS/P. Maitre.

Printed and bound in Europe by Arvato Iberia
Colour separations: Station Graphique, Ivry-sur-Seine

617-015-02